Prai[se]

With Hodge's calm, [...] [tha]t this young man went through to become the role model that he is today. Truth is stranger than fiction, which is clearly demonstrated in *Chum Water*. Can't wait for the sequel. ~ Sharon Sanderson, MPH, OTR/L, FAOTA, Professor Emeritus, Oklahoma University Health Sciences Center, and President, Oklahoma Occupational Therapy Association

Chum Water is a contemporary masterpiece. Hodge has been my friend since we wrestled together each weighing sixty pounds. His life story with its ups and downs makes you laugh, cry, squirm and applaud. This is a common man with uncommon problems and the intestinal fortitude to slay the dragons in his path. When the neurosurgeon said he would never walk again, Hodge had a choice to make. He chose to ignore the negativity of his life and realize that God had something more important for him . . . I highly recommend this book to anyone who has had a 'crisis' in his life. So that through Hodge's example, we will know that God exists and has a purpose for each of us. ~ John Powers Clemons, M.D., Midwest Regional Medical Center, Midwest City, Oklahoma

BRAVO! Great Story. I knew the Big Picture, but now that I know the details, I am certainly impressed. I always felt that if anyone could recover from such a devastating injury, it is Hodge Wood. Hodge is the most positive individual that I know and I have to believe that this attitude played a major role in his recovery. He has the rare knack of making you feel that you are worth a zillion bucks. The world would be a much better place if there were more folks like Hodge! ~ Russ Tribble MCHS BOMBER Football Teammate, Arkansas Razorbacks 1975 SWC Champs, College/HS Football Coach

Chum Water is an intriguing story of a young man at the peak of physical prowess who is involved in an accident that leaves him totally helpless and completely at the mercy of others. In his struggles for survival, Hodge experiences the worst and the best of the VA health care system. As he navigates the system, he is stripped of his dignity and self respect until a PA becomes aware of his situation and takes charge. Through the care and friendship of Mike Kuns—and the courage and determination of Hodge himself, we see a life transformed from one of complete helplessness to one who would become an occupational therapist and devote his life to giving help and hope to others. ~ **Eddie R. Beesley, author of** *Lucky Enough*

Amazing! I couldn't put it down! A journey through spiritual, physical and mental rehabilitation and growth. I loved every bit of it . . . even the painful parts. I experienced every emotion one could have—sadness, empathy, joy, laughter, anger—and could relate to so much because those were my times too! ~ **Janet Eskridge, Registered Physical Therapist**

I have read Hodge Wood's book *Chum Water* with much interest. As a quadriplegic myself, Hodge's book gives the reader a glimpse into the life of someone whose life has been battered but not beaten. Someone who was independent and at one time thought of themselves as ten feet tall and bulletproof, but now has to rely on others. Someone though disabled, not unable. Someone, whose life has been changed 180 degrees, but still has hopes and dreams, never stops hoping, and never stops dreaming. To sum up my view and to interject a couple of quotes: "Where there's a will there is a way" and "I have a dream." ~ **Bill Kokendoffer, President, Mid- America Chapter, Paralyzed Veterans of America**

Chum Water is an absolutely mesmerizing account of a man losing his life as he knew it only to become a whole man through learning how to live again after a tragic spinal cord injury and paralysis. As a speech-language pathologist working in a rehab setting for over thirty years, Hodge's story of courage and determination touched me to the depths of my soul. I will never treat another patient quite the same again. Knowing Hodge in our early formative years through high school and keeping in touch briefly through the years, I had no idea the challenges he faced. My heart swells with pride and admiration for him as I read his brilliant and amazing tale of how he met his demons and conquered them through sheer strength, belief in himself and his faith in God. ~ **Jeanette Winkcomplexk Clemons, MA CCC-SLP, Speech-Language Pathologist, Midwest Regional Medical Center, Midwest City, Oklahoma**

Sharks On Wounded Fish

Chum Water

Dear Beth,
UR A Wonderful
Soul :)
Thanks for Supporting
our work
Hope Wood

Sharks On Wounded Fish

Chum Water

by
Hodge Wood

River Road Press
Laguna Vista, Texas

Published by *River Road Press*,
an imprint of **Red Engine Press**

Copyright © 2007 by Hodge Wood

All Rights Reserved. No part of this book may be reproduced or transmitted in any form or by any means, electronic or mechanical, including photocopying, recording, or by an information storage and retrieval system (except by a reviewer who may quote brief passages in a review to be printed in a magazine, newspaper or on the Internet) without permission in writing from the publisher.

Library of Congress Control Number: 2007924726

ISBN: 978-0-9785158-6-7

Photos from Hodge Wood

Edited by RRP Consulting

Printed in the United States of America

Quantity discounts are available on bulk purchases of this book for educational institutions or social organizations. For information, please contact the publisher:
River Road Press
13 Torrey Pines Drive
Laguna Vista, TX 78578

Dedication

I dedicate my book series to a former medic from Vietnam named Mike Kuns. He took charge of my care at the VA Medical Center in Oklahoma City three decades ago and saved my life. Mike continues to serve at this center in a way that is honorable and selfless. Few are dedicated like Mike, and I thank him for his compassion, skill, and unrelenting leadership.

Mike, you are the best care provider I have met in my thirty-year experience as a patient and occupational therapist. You told me way back during my first two months of hospitalization that I should write a book. So, here it is.

Acknowledgments

To my sweet wife Beth—thank you for the time and support to write this story. Your patience never ends. I know the sacrifices for me take time and energy that you could use in relaxing ways. I owe you ten thousand favors.

To my "Book Shepherd" Joyce Faulkner—thank you for your caring professional assistance. I have grown in leaps and bounds from the education given. Your advice comes with a trusting smile every time, and you never cease to amaze me. You never quit and it's a pleasure to be on your team.

Contents

Foreword	xi
Introduction	xiii
One ~ Gaffed	1
Disco Fever	1
Running with the Devil	5
Dying Minnow in the Bucket	8
Two ~ Gutted	10
Live Well	10
On the Stringer	11
Guardian Angel Arrives	15
Dental Hygiene Therapist	17
Nowhere to Go but Up	17
Gradation	20
The Way We Were	22
Occupational Therapy	23
Living in Homer's Frame	25
Generate Income	26
Torture Time	27
Cada Coda	28
Hired Help Could Kill You	30
Machismo Act	32
Dream to Walk, Live to Bleed	33
Own Football Stadium	35
A Piece of Cake	37
Level Playing Field	38
Flying First Class	40
Spare Parts	41
Bowel Training Class	42
Cowboys on the Cattle Drive	44
A Fish Returns to Water	48

Three ~ Stink Bait... 52
    Outside the Bars.. 52
    Football Mentality Meets Shrinker............................. 52
    Taped Up To Play.. 56
    Identity Crisis... 59
    Revised Agenda... 61
    Running On Empty.. 63
    Crazy on You... 63
    What to Do?... 65
    Disability Took Nothing Away.................................. 67

Four ~ Nursing.. 69
    Jet on a Jaguar... 69
    Dumb as a Rock.. 72
    Carefree Energy... 74
    Back in the Saddle Again.. 75
    Crash Course.. 77
    Save My Life.. 79
    More Faster.. 80
    Funky King.. 84
    Boiling Chemicals... 88
    Licking Wounds Clean.. 90

Five ~ Schooling.. 93
    Making the Cut... 93
    Not Kansas Anymore.. 94
    Lab Orientation... 98
    Fishing Around... 100
    Healing Power... 103
    Out of My League... 104
    Cadaver Lives.. 105
    Last Ride.. 106
    Don't Wake Me... 107
    Back to Blue Water... 112
    Spontaneous Thermodynamics.............................. 116
    Get Back In Line... 118
    Hooked On Love... 120
    Sharp Blade... 122
    Ordinary.. 123

    Rich.. 124
    Cock of the Walk... 128
    Keep the Corks... 130
    Intellectual Currents.. 133
    Nice Church Wedding... 135
    Bathrooms in Paradise.. 139
Six ~ Sea World...145
    Patrol the Captured... 145
    Where I Came From.. 147
    Where I Was Going... 150
    Galaxy.. 154
    Game to Try.. 155
    Bone Deep... 157
    Back At the Ranch... 160
    Walter's Night Out... 162
    Male Marlin... 163
    Follow the Red Dots.. 166
Index...170

Foreword

There was that guy I'd seen before—peering through the ropes into my world. He was a slender athlete sporting a short beard. The cowboy shirt and Wrangler jeans labeled him a south-sider. With cane in hand, he limped and stumbled in as he glanced to see if he blocked someone's view while finding his seat. He was always on front row-center. His entrance made a scene. Who was this mystery man? Why does he like boxing? Why does he limp?

After my fights he hung around with the crowd to say hello and pay his respects. We engaged in conversation but, unlike many others, he listened. What did he want? He seemed to know a lot about boxing, sports, and even a lot about me. We found a common interest; water skiing. Water skiing? WATER SKIING? He said he could. This I had to see!

Out of coincidence on a frigid February day in 1982, we had heard of a lake heated by a hydro-electric plant that could be skied on. Our fate crossed paths. With only two boats on water as cold as the North Pole, I finally began to really know Hodge Wood. We had much in common. The friendship evolved to last a lifetime.

At first I inquired about his limp, his cane and his difficulty in maneuvering. He told me stories that enabled me to be a better champion. I realized how effective the power of concentration can be and how to focus on long range goals, ignoring the little negative bumps in the road. Over many dinners, we discussed how much life mirrors sport—and specifically boxing. Like an older brother I never had, Hodge taught me about positive mental attitude. He used the same warped sense of humor that I did. In life's battles, he knew to keep his head down and hands up. When backed into a corner, he had fought like a trapped cat. I learned a lot about myself and a lot about character from him.

Hodge and I talked about self-reliance, responsibility and that there are no shortcuts. We discussed training and the solitude of my life as an athlete, and he shared how it related to his ongoing recovery. Hodge said to finish commitments and never quit — especially when alone, so as to serve others better. Our discussions of faith ran deep. We valued the presence of a divine spirit and the need to turn to the bible and prayer. He taught me a lot about right and wrong.

Hodge continues to enlighten me about love when I see him with his family. I feel like part of their clan. His wife Beth is a dear friend, and their boys Cody and Dalton are young champs. Although stern and steadfast, Hodge's compassion runs deep and he can laugh at his shortcomings. To help people, he became an occupational therapist for twenty years with the alacrity of a young athlete. Hodge tried to learn all there was to know, gave more back and remained cheerful throughout even the most trying times. As an athlete, I appreciate this dedication.

His is a humorous, no nonsense story of courage, strength, and perseverance — he pulls no punches. From humble beginnings to the roller coaster of life, Hodge Wood has character. To read this book is to know Hodge Wood. And to know Hodge Wood is to know character.

    Sean O'Grady

    1981 WBA Lightweight World Champion

    1992 Inductee - Boxing Hall of Fame

    2003 Inductee - Oklahoma Sports Hall of Fame

    TV Sports Color Commentator/Broadcaster

Introduction

Chum Water is the first book from my *Sharks on Wounded Fish* series. It is about a common man entering a complex world. After a near fatal accident, I spent life as a patient and health care provider. This book reveals those first four eventful years.

This personal memoir is for those who like humor and perseverance. The inner self reveals the positive and negative, what we are and who we become when we lose and gain. *Chum Water* begins a journey with a man who has no fancy side. I seek the Lord and regret when I've run with the devil. God's spirit leads us through the beautiful and humorous, as well as the tragic and terrifying. I remain in awe at how He pulls us out of every jam. Through His grace I live to share why I am a lucky man and true street survivor.

Names were changed — including my patients — for reasons of confidentiality.

For a just man falleth seven times, and riseth up again:
but the wicked shall fall into mischief.

Proverbs 24:16 (KJV)

Hodge - 1977

One ~ Gaffed

Disco Fever

A hot shower capped off the workday. I paused naked to gaze through the bathroom window and absorb the fresh air. The fragrance of soap mixed with the smell of grass and the sounds of play from Walter, my basset hound. The late October afternoon felt pleasant, but I sensed an unusual stillness of the wind. The calm silence seemed mysterious as I dried off.

I slipped a T-shirt that read SKOAL BROTHER over my stomach grid and strapped up coveralls. In the mirror, my callused fingertips grazed the sides of the fu-manchu mustache that wrapped around the corners of my mouth. The reflection showed the back of my right arm. I flexed it to see all three muscles bulge. In terrific shape at twenty-four, I felt great. No one could beat me.

Heading for the bedroom, I jumped up to touch the top of the door frame with my toe—something I did from time to time for fun. I was going out to hear a traveler play guitar at Twentieth Century Electric Light Company. I laughed at the irony of me sitting in a disco club to hear a folk singer. The disco fad went full swing in 1977, but it suffered in Oklahoma. For this I was thankful. Tonight the disco club offered all the draft beer you could drink and the show for five bucks. What a ridiculous promo. They expected a full house and I would make them pay by sucking down my share of a keg. In my mind, I would make money on the deal.

I shadowboxed into the living room, thumbed through the records and found an album by my favorite band. Lynyrd Skynyrd came to life with the volume cranked. "Whiskey Rock-A-Roller" blasted through the speakers and pumped me sky-high.

Hodge Wood

Back in my room, I put on a necklace of wood beads and pulled up my Wellington boots. I was still uneasy. Maybe the eerie feeling was because some fool had kicked my back door in a month ago. I started to conceal my pistol, decided not to and laid the weapon back down next to the bed. Why the uncommon fright? Maybe the evening disco destination put me far out of my water. I squared my cowboy hat and took one last look in the mirror. From my upbringing on the street, I recognized a survival instinct in the eyes staring back at me—fear.

Barbara and I lived together and she treated me well. Japanese ancestry gave her beautiful oriental features like black hair and almond eyes. She was quiet like her dad, Jimmy. Barb needed more of my attention, but I would deal with it later. My pickup had broken down so I borrowed Jimmy's car. It ran well but looked like a beater. The window wouldn't roll up but this wasn't a problem as the fall weather was perfect. I snuck off after dark driving more careful than normal. I had never had any wrecks or tickets, but it was important not to damage Jimmy's car. He was kind to loan it.

Thoughts came to my mind about past passenger misfortunes. I flashed back to the night a drunk hit us head-on. I was six years old. We were in my brother John's '58 Impala, cruising at fifty-five, when the drunk crossed three lanes in a drag race and smashed into us. John ran the metal steering column through the dash, my sister-in-law busted her feet and she held their baby in the car seat. The collision threw me out into the darkness. John's car slammed sideways and almost ran over me. Lying on the four-lane, I reached around my left arm and felt holes in my sleeve. Debris was strewn all over the street. The black skid marks on my torn jacket sleeve revealed how close the tire came as the car careened out of control an instant earlier. The concrete had sheared the hair off the side of my head. Crushed bongo drums were at my feet. Seconds before, the plant-filled bongos sat between my legs in the front seat and now they were gone. John's car raced at full throttle in the ditch.

Chum Water

Wow—Stop—Hold your horses! My mind returned to the present. I chilled out and thought of the positive. I had survived that wreck and many rough times on the street. Always a hard worker, my reputation was being honest and disciplined, staying the course and getting things done. People knew I never quit.

Tonight felt spooky. Sensing the radio would distract me, I reached for the knob and turned it on, but it didn't play. As the club came into sight, I groaned and thought, "Here it is, Twentieth Century Electric Light Company. Would anyone mistake me for a disco boy?" The thought made me shudder. Jimmy's car wouldn't lock but there wasn't much to vandalize. Man, my senses were keen. What was it? I needed to down a few draws and mellow out. I entered the club eager to get my five dollars worth.

A Bee Gee's tune from *Saturday Night Fever* ruined a great sound system. They had to be steers to sing that high. The movie was okay, but I passed on the canned music created with electronic gizmos. The fake disco scene left me cold—no rhythm or blues. Feed me ZZ Top, thank you. The light show wasted electricity. I tried to fit in as the resident animals in the zoo exited. They had noticed that their habitat was experiencing a makeover for the evening. Instead of the regular crowd, God's peculiar people came out. I watched a couple of rough characters counseling the DJ in the sound booth. Lest his thumbs be broken, he created an atmosphere other than disco.

He played something bearable and I danced. Moving with the coordination and strength of a tribesman, I enjoyed my primitive side in an acceptable way. I had endless endurance. Dancing, like boxing, requires you to get off to be good. I got off and was good. The beer and the dance blended to compose what felt right. I made movement and floated in a trance. At my age, I loved being physical and depended on it for security.

Soon the place was hopping. I knew to stay close to my chair up front or I might have to bounce someone out of it. Refreshed by the dance and draft, I sat down as the folk singer began his first set.

I caught eyes with the cowboy to my left. He was rowdy and chased the girls like a buck deer in rut. His dark eyes seemed friendly but he looked drunk. I downed a pitcher and gained comfort in thinking that he wouldn't turn his obnoxious behavior my way. Strange—I sensed that he recognized me.

"Do I know ya?" he asked.

"Maybe, I don't know."

We entered into small talk. He said he remembered a brief meeting in a crowded house. I couldn't recall it but knew his voice. We figured out we used to work for the same stereo sales company.

"Remember talking on the phone about shipping stereo gear from one store to another?" I asked.

My statement tied us together like long-lost friends. He slapped me across the back and responded, "Yeeehaaahhh! Damn, I know ya!"

The live band started and I shook hands with Dave Washington. We were two peas in a pod. Bottoms up, we drank our bellies' full. I tended to take risks—an admitted weakness. This night, my risk-taking trait established precedence over my dominant habit of using common sense. I joined the "Fools Brigade."

Dave needed supervision. I took on the role and figured everyone was relieved. I didn't like the way he behaved but under the beer's intoxication, I tolerated it. Dave loved to hug my neck and I never denied affection. He made it to the stage and placed his ten-gallon hat on the singer's head, which was funny to the crowd. However, it didn't take long for Dave to alienate everyone in the place. The show ended and I considered my escape for home. Dave invited me to another bar. Who was I to deny such an offer? Dave took a partial pitcher to go. The bouncers at the door accepted the loss of a large glass mug as the cost of doing business and chose not to fight.

Running with the Devil

In the starlight, I noticed Dave's full-sized Dodge van had a faded custom paint job. Dave almost started a fight with someone. I warned him to cut the crap and brooded over what I was doing, running with this man. We crawled into his van with nothing to say. I sensed the devil was present as I looked across the countryside. The stars were brilliant and antenna lights reached to the sky. I had never been where we were and did not know where we were going. The moonless night scared me. I leaned back and listened to the radio. Demons were around and life was not that meaningful. Besides, I was fit and could take care of myself—that was my security.

A radio report stunned me. The Lynyrd Skynyrd Band crashed in an airplane and all may have died. The exact list of the deceased was unknown.

My fear was intense. I felt the loss of close brothers and sisters and wanted to go home as Dave pulled into a bar parking lot. Sobered by the news, I finally understood my fear of the evening. The devil had joined us and put his arm around me.

I didn't want to go into the club but Dave insisted we would have fun. He fooled around with the few in attendance but I kept my distance from him. I closed down emotionally and listened to the guitar player singing a Jimmy Buffett song, "Come Monday." The music soothed my restless soul. I learned that the list of dead Skynyrd players included Ronnie Van Zant, the lead singer and Steve Gaines from Oklahoma. The guitar player offered to let me strum his guitar and I picked a crude chord rendition of "Free Bird" in dedication to the deceased Skynyrd members. My heart was broken over their crash.

Dave switched to hard liquor. I had nothing and wanted to go home. Finally, I made Dave leave. The parking area was empty and the night was still and creepy. I slid into Dave's van. Dave first tried to drive over a parked car. I threatened him with violence if he did and could have cold cocked him from the side with a right lead, but held it back. He dropped the plan.

We again had nothing to say. I fixed on getting to Jimmy's car. I wanted to feel the cool air blow through the window that would not roll up as I steered home to lie in bed with Barbara. I prayed to God to get me home and forgive me for acting like a fool in the first place. I imagined Barb's warm, naked touch. The cool morning air would awaken us to another day. Home wasn't too far away.

Dave backed out and floored it. He sped off into the country. I was lost. Dave refused to listen to my warnings to slow down and instead sped up. Silence took command over words. Four-way stop signs in each valley divided the wooded hills. Dave chose to speed through a couple of the intersections, turning his headlights off to look for oncoming light beams before blasting through.

Dave came to a stop—then laid rubber to the right. He accelerated. Ahead, I saw a bridge. The overpass curved hard to the left.

It felt like I was on a state fair ride, except not by choice. Being a motocross rider prepared me to fall. The speedometer slipped past sixty-five. The bridge girder beams ahead were made of steel reinforced concrete. Dave never let off the gas pedal.

We slammed into the bridge with horrific force. The collision made a hideous sound—an amplified clatter of iron and metal meeting unmovable stone. The demonic noise penetrated the cab. The front of the van bent under my seat as the windshield burst out from my boots that rose to stop the impact. The van flipped end over end several times. Suspended in time, I thought that I'd be fine once the van stopped moving.

Upside down, the roof scraped against the pavement. The noise was deafening. The van leaped back over into an upright position and flew through the air in complete silence. We went over again. The van tore apart and hammered me faster than my protective reflexes could react. I hurled forward like a baseball from the back of the van and my arms were not fast enough to reach ahead. My forehead struck the top of the Dodge that was bending inward against the concrete and it snapped my head backwards.

I heard a loud crack and saw stars. From then on, it felt like my body was tucked into a mattress. The pummeling forces caused no pain. I bashed around the interior as the van spun and slid across the pavement. I had no feeling of the glass and metal that penetrated and punished my body.

The van halted upside down. I lay face down in the back. Adrenaline shot through my body and warned me to move. The wreckage smelled hot and I needed to get out before it caught on fire. My cowboy hat had crushed down over my eyes and it blocked most of my vision. I attempted to jump up and run but could not get off my face. I couldn't breathe. Terrified, I tried harder to bolt, like any wounded animal would try to do.

Nothing moved and I couldn't feel anything. My mind glimpsed the past when I was tackled and wrenched my neck in a high school football game. I couldn't move at first but later I got up. Now I was far worse. My neck was broken—my body paralyzed. I cried to God for help and forgiveness, accepted that I might die and hoped He would still take me into His kingdom. The circumstances that surrounded my impending departure shook me and I had great fear of the Lord. I thought how dumb I was to let this happen. I surfed my mind for all those who loved me and about all the beautiful things I had. Now they would be hurt or gone because I didn't have enough sense to keep from snapping my neck. I continued to try to get my cowboy hat off but could not. Lying on my face, I struggled to breathe. Survival was the priority.

A distant siren broke the absolute silence. The sound grew louder as the ambulance came for me. I never again saw Dave Washington. He left the state after getting out of jail. He had no insurance. He knew he had maimed me—and ran.

My life had changed forever.

Dying Minnow in the Bucket

It shocked me when the policewoman got my ID. I never felt her hands in my pockets. The ambulance crew said nothing, sandbagged my head and delivered me to an observation room.

I couldn't wipe my tears without arms or hands. To inhale any oxygen at all took a constant, conscious effort. My body didn't move but gravity pushed it firmly against the treatment table. The exam room was sterile. I had never been hospitalized and didn't know what to expect, but I knew the future was not bright.

A young doctor came in and asked questions without any other interaction. "Do you feel this? Which toe do I have?" He went on.

I did not have a clue and he left without saying anything.

My family came in the room, looking sorrowful. The pain in their eyes was worse than anything else. How could I have done this? What do I say? My dad could not grasp what happened. My sister didn't sleep for seven days. I prayed for God to help me be strong for them.

The next ambulance took me to St. Anthony's Hospital. They wobbled me around to tug off my coveralls. My Wellington boots were gone. The people at the first hospital took them off and I never felt it. I had no sensation at all.

"Are you on drugs?" Someone asked.

"No, just beer," I said.

No further conversation transpired. No comforting took place. There was no encouragement. As a black man cut my SKOAL BROTHER T-shirt off, I looked to see if he saw the printed humor but he didn't smile. I looked into his face as he spoke. "I will place the catheter in your penis."

I did not feel the catheter and watched him pump the bulb up inside my bladder. My heart burst. My physical security was gone. The black man left without words.

Neurosurgeon Rhinehart came in. He put his fists on top of one another and then bent them apart as he said, "You broke your neck and will never walk again. I will move you to the Veterans Hospital ICU."

The doctor spoke in a matter-of-fact way and then left without another word. I could tell he was upset and figured I was just another scumbag with no future who had gotten him out of bed. I understood. He left so fast I didn't get a chance to apologize.

A stooge can't expect treatment like a guest at the Holiday Inn, but questions hit me. Why was everybody so cold? Will anyone talk? How does a hospital help with an attitude of indifference and apparent dislike for me? Do they know that I am sorry? Do they know who I am? Do they realize I am scared and need hope? Do they care for me? I didn't think so. The indifference weighed heavily on me. I wanted out. I was another speared fish caught without care, stabbed and thrown in a pile—helpless. I was one of many in their care.

I had been gaffed.

Two ~ Gutted

Live Well

The ambulance pulled out and bounced me across town to the VA Hospital. My head banged around like a pinball steely. Neck pain stabbed me with each jarring motion. I cried out, "Please bag my head better — Oh, God — the sandbags are loose!" The two attendants stared at me but never responded.

They rolled me inside on a gurney. I counted ceiling tiles as we went towards the ICU, smelled cigarettes and passed Mr. Morgan. Did I imagine him? He was the strong father of my close childhood friend, Mark. I was exhausted and faded.

In my mind I rode again, after grade school, in the back of Mr. Morgan's bread delivery truck. Mark and the other boys were with me. Football practice had worked up our appetites and sometimes we got a cupcake. I could smell the fresh pastry and bread in Mr. Morgan's route truck. Mr. Morgan got up at two each morning to deliver bread. I wanted to grow up and work that hard and be that good. Mr. Morgan offered us each a banana cream-filled snack and we ate the fresh treat. The boy's laughter was contagious. Without a care, we poked at each other in the bread truck.

My vision broke with the reality of my new hospital placement. The ICU was busy and I gazed around at the monitors, my urine bag and IV. My spinal cord had swollen and the steroids were being administered. The spinal injury nauseated me and I began to vomit. They rushed to roll me over then and often after that. I couldn't move and they wouldn't let me eat. I was suspended in an unending twenty-four hour schedule of dependency with a panoramic view of harsh reality.

An old man ran by two days later. He yelled, "Yoooohhh! Yoooohhh!" His torso flew behind the rolling IV pole that he pushed. It was hooked to a line that terminated in his arm. He had pulled the plugs on his other monitors and his nose tube was still dangling. It was the middle of the night. A stream of nurses urged him to stop and return to bed. From my position, the chase looked odd. The old man and nurses circled around my corner of the ICU floor. They zoomed by bodies lying in the pits at the edge of an impromptu human racetrack. After the excitement was over, the nurses laid the old man down and he died. I could not see him, but heard him give up the ghost and the commotion to save and later remove him.

Later, an ICU staff nurse who had befriended me came over, picked up my hand and held it. I sensed how bad she hurt for the old man who had passed on, but she first asked if I was okay. I told the nurse that I was sorry that he had died and that I recognized how much they did for us here. I asked, "How do you take it?"

She wept and I wished that I could hold her. She soon recovered with a smile and I was impressed with her resilience. She talked about her two children and I commented about them as we let the event pass.

On the Stringer

Days passed. People leaned over me and gave me instructions. Everyone was in my personal space and each possessed authority.

The respiratory therapist above me said, "Since you can't move or sit, your lungs are filling up. I am going to place this tube down your nose and suction them. You will have to help me."

"Help you?" I asked, hoping to negotiate out.

"Yes, just open and swallow," she replied.

I tried and tried and tried. The tube went down my nose and came back out of my mouth. I couldn't help but laugh once I caught my breath.

"I will be back often," she noted, leaving me with a breathing exercise device that I used religiously.

"Time to change your catheter," the next person leaned over and said.

Another peered over me. "Your bowels haven't moved since you have been here and you are impacted. I'm gonna roll ya' over and place in a suppository." Over I went without responding.

I felt strange saying anything—but I did anyway. "I am hungry," I said to a nurse. She looked at me and answered. "You can't eat by mouth, just through your IV."

But I could.

I said, "Oh yes, please, I can eat by mouth." I injected a little humor. "How will you get steak and potatoes through that IV, anyway?" I could tell she was not impressed or swayed, so I continued using manners. "I am sincere. Please let me have something to eat. I haven't eaten since the afternoon before I was hurt."

Please and thank you didn't carry any weight. "You have to have a doctor's order to eat by mouth."

I was honest and determined. "Where is he and when can I see him? I want to eat so I can get well."

Before walking away, the nurse said in closing, "You are scheduled for a myelogram and he will do it."

I wondered, "What is a myelogram?"

It was strange to be paralyzed. I thought about my numerous hired visitors who walked up and looked down at me before proceeding to do something to my body and give orders. I had never asked for anything in life and was fierce about being independent. I got by on my own and always worked a full day, but now I was a high maintenance item. For several days, every orifice on my body had been violated—but my mouth seemed to have a "No Food Allowed" sign posted on it. Most queer to me was that nobody took the cue to call me Hodge. If anyone called me by name, they called me William, my first name. I never went by that name in my life. It felt impersonal. Each time I said to the same people and to the new ones, "My name is Hodge," nobody ever caught the cue. How peculiar, I was William.

My skin began to break down on both of my heels, as I was not turned often enough and pressure sores developed. My bowels moved without any feeling of urge. I had no control—if by chance they didn't move, the staff used fingers or meds. I burned like I had been placed in ice up to my chest. Although trapped in a body that did not move, my mind was clear. Around the clock, I listened and lived.

My mother fed me ice chips when she got off work from the bakery. Two family members or friends could visit every two hours for ten minutes—visiting hour policy. I developed admiration for the ICU staff for they were skilled in managing tragedies. However, I was unaware of many developments. My family voiced concerns over arising issues—like my skin breaking down because the staff failed to turn my paralyzed body, as they were required to do. The ICU staff got upset with them for complaining and asked them to leave. My sister Bev was willing to help the physical therapist who had been teaching her to range my extremities and to promote returned movement. However, nursing wasn't supportive. Bev thought they cared less if I recovered and wondered why they didn't admire my positive attitude and willingness to get well. They did not—and that hurt her. I had never been lonelier and people were everywhere.

Twenty-four hours a day in ICU lets the mind wander, reflect and worry. Others placed a radio headset on me. Within the first week, a somber radio voice introduced the new Lynyrd Skynyrd *Street Survivors* album. The cut, "What's That Smell" filled my ears for the first time. Skynyrd's lyrics opened with "whiskey bottles—and brand new cars—oak tree you're in my way." Death was and had been near me. Its closeness made my body ache with emotion. I threw up without a word. Skynyrd's message was to avoid the excesses, but their warning was too late for me to heed. Reality was too much. Forever scarred, I lay alone gathering up everlasting changes. I was a good man in bad shape.

LYNYRD SKYNYRD

STREET SURVIVORS
1977 WINTER TOUR
Watch Newspapers for Show Dates

Dr. Schoenhals, the Chief Resident of Neurosurgery, was my VA assigned personal physician. A husky man, he heralded his arrival to perform my myelogram by throwing chairs and scaring the hired help for their inattention to his needs. As Schoenhals started the procedure, he busted a plastic glove and swore. Then he became as cool as a western gunfighter. He palpated below my ear where my neck had been shaved. As if aiming a rifle, he stared below my ear and asked the staff for a large needle. He aimed the dye-filled syringe at my neck and said, "Hold still. I will put this through your neck into your spinal cord."

I affirmed him by saying, "I'm in good hands, Doc," and projected myself out of my body a million miles away.

Dr. Schoenhals said, "Hodge, to do this you have to have your shit together."

I was sure he did — and he called me Hodge, which was comforting. The needle penetrated into my neck and spinal cord. They rolled me around and got pictures of the spinal damage that the dye revealed.

Before Schoenhals left I said, "Doc, I know I am in bad shape but I am hungry and could eat a real meal and be stronger and recover faster. They said you would have to order that. Also, I know I am in ICU but the Sooners are playing football on TV Saturday and I want to watch the game. They said there is no way in ICU — but they can put me anywhere I can see a TV. Please?"

He stared at me and said, "You will have it." He left.

It created a stir, but I got three square meals a day from then on and the staff plugged in a TV right in the middle of the ICU floor so I could watch every Sooner game. It turned out that Schoenhals was a big Sooner football fan himself — and he provided direct support to the program. I was ecstatic. It might seem a small thing, but the food strengthened my body and the Sooners gave me something to focus on besides my own sorry situation.

Guardian Angel Arrives

The most respectable health care provider I ever met came to see me. He had met my family and said they were nice people. He told me hard work was required. I had no problem with that. He said,

"You and your family have had problems here that I will do all I can to resolve. I will help you with anything else you need. I am Mike Kuns, Physician Assistant and I look forward to managing your care plan—you can ask for me and count on me." Mike said all of that in just his introduction. My guardian angel had arrived.

Mike provided an ear and honest advice for the millions of thoughts and problems I had. Although he worked late every day, Mike was always genuine to me. He gave me time and respect— and he believed in me. When things came up, Mike went to bat for me. His desire and sincerity to serve his fellow veteran started in the jungles of Vietnam, as a field medic. I trusted him. We laughed and cried together—and I never met another who served so well.

"Mike," I asked, "What will happen? Can you give me a step by step idea?"

He told me that Dr. Schoenhals needed to place me in traction and that screws inserted in my head would attach to traction tongs. The staff would place me into a Stryker Frame—a device that allows for turning to avoid skin pressure sores. The tongs would have 20 pounds of weight pulling on them to reduce compression on my spinal cord. I would be turned every two hours to face down, then four hours to face up—for several weeks. At that time, the doctor would consider fusing my fractured C5 - C6 vertebrae. In a couple of months, Mike was going to arrange to have me flown air medevac to the Veterans Spinal Cord Injury Service in Memphis, Tennessee. Mike said that he would keep in touch with my team and see me when I came home to arrange outpatient care and decide where and how I would live.

I appreciated his detailed description. "Mike, they told my family to find a nursing home with twenty-four hour care. What do you think?"

"I think it is too early to tell." He paused before continuing, "It's up to the good Lord and you. Do your best, Hodge, that's all anyone can do."

I had to tell him, "Mike, I moved the fingers of my left hand a little yesterday. They said it was spasticity—but I moved them."

"If you know you moved them," he said, "that is the greatest thing I could hear. It is very promising."

"I will keep working every minute," I promised. I also told him that my physical therapist came in after he clocked out to teach my sister Beverly how to help—and she did!

Dental Hygiene Therapist

Beverly worked in a dental office. The staff, saying it was slow, would send her to help her brother. She was refused entry into ICU except for ten minutes at visiting time. Finally, Sis came up with a plan to break the ten-minute rule. She put her lab coat on with her name tag from the dental office. Then she placed the physical therapy handouts that they gave her onto a clipboard, strolled through the ICU doors, assumed a staff appearance and went to work ranging me out. The first day her heart pumped out of her chest. Day two, she was less anxious. Day three, no one had yet to say anything, so she gained confidence incognito as a therapist.

One day the medical students were on rounds as Bev worked with me. A curious female student observed Sis and asked what she was doing.

Bev responded, "Therapy."

The student said, "RDH—doesn't your name tag stand for Registered Dental Hygienist?"

Bev said, "Yes and you better shut up."

The student said, "I understand." She smiled and departed.

Nowhere to Go but Up

The crackling of skull bone amplified through my head as the screws were twisted into place. The skull conducts as part of the hearing system. I couldn't believe how loud it was. Bone dust filled my nostrils. The drilling and screwing progressed. As they attached the tongs, I focused on the good news. I would not have to stay in ICU anymore and that meant progress.

The orderly rolled me upstairs to Ward 7 North, the Neuro Ward and transferred me on my back into a Stryker frame. They took the top of the frame and placed it on my front side and secured it with various tighteners at the ends of the frame. This allowed my chin to rest upon a strap. I could see between it and another strap across my forehead. The attending staff coordinated a roll. Suddenly, I was face down on my stomach to remove pressure from my backside. The floor looked much different from the ceiling. I had no image of my body. They attached twenty pounds of traction plates on a rope that hooked into the tongs that locked to the screws that protruded above my ears. The back compartment of the Stryker was unscrewed and removed. I listened but could not see the attachments come out. Someone laid the back of the frame down and everyone left.

It was scary looking through the straps at the ground, unable to look in either direction. I got cold. The ward was much quieter than the ICU but conversations far away could be overheard. I tried to envision what the Stryker looked like and wondered what the area looked like that surrounded me.

Barbara ducked under the frame, gave me a kiss and smiled up at me. Other family members and friends followed and did the same—not limited to two at a time. I felt like the oil pan bolt on the bottom of a car engine as everybody crawled under to see me. They could now stay longer than ten minutes, which was great. Yes, this was progress.

After my visitors had left, I watched roaches crawl across the floor underneath me. Although the staff placed a blanket on me, I was freezing and my teeth chattered. I looked at the call button down in front of me. My working biceps and shoulders could not coordinate my paralyzed hand to grasp it. I shouted for help and waited. Again and again, I called and waited. I could hear the nursing staff talking—could smell their cigarettes for several smokes, but there was no response to my pleas for assistance.

Finally, an attending staff arrived and said in a mean voice, "Just what do YOU want?"

I hesitated, then said, "a blanket, please."

She left.

I waited—cold and alone.

Much later she raced by and threw another blanket on me. "You have to realize that we make rounds."

"B-but --," I stammered.

"You'll just have to accept that you'll get what you need then," she said over her shoulder as she disappeared down the hall.

I had a hollow feeling and a lump in my throat.

I wanted security—the one thing I couldn't have. Tears hit the ground below. What I had depended on most—my physical strength—was now gone. I prayed for the courage to keep trying—but that night, I felt abandoned.

I was too cold to sleep. There was a simple solution—the blanket should have been placed underneath me. All that guarded me from the chill below was the canvas frame. It was weeks later, after being removed from the Stryker, before I finally got warm. A deeper, bigger picture came to my mind. How many others across the years had also frozen in the Stryker? Why had professional health care staff not analyzed this need for a blanket underneath? I chalked up these notes on what would later be an extended list of "systematic" failures within the health care system.

Barb and Bev camped out each night in the waiting room area to try to insure that the orderlies properly turn me. Hospital rules wouldn't allow Barb and Bev to stay on the ward overnight—but because they were nearby and in communication with Mike Kuns, the heat stayed on. Their dedication was modestly successful. I was turned enough to survive, but not enough to keep my skin from breaking down. Bev believed that they would not have turned me once without family there. The staff had already written me off—so what if my skin sloughed off?

The doctors and therapists were in constant battles with the nursing staff over my care. Bev came one evening during visiting hours and could not find a single employee on the entire floor. She searched bathrooms, throughout the Neuro ward and on the Chemical Dependency Unit—everywhere. My family fought with staff members who were not shy about revealing that they didn't like caring for patients like me.

Gradation

My body was foreign and had to be assessed each day. Gravity continued to keep me from moving despite my constant attempts to focus and move every part. After the first few days, I could rub my left big toe, which had some motion, against my right one that would not move. Both toes felt abnormal—but they had some sort of feeling again. I could bite parts of my arms and hands and differentiate the anesthetized areas from those in which I had some feeling again. Mark Morgan inspired me to succeed in pulling a Kleenex out of the box with my left hand—a task I had tried to master for hours each day. The catheters were beginning to hurt when they were placed in—but more on my right side. Spasms in my right arm and leg were greater. I kept track of a million small details—marking each change in status as the weeks passed.

My automatic lights were stuck in the on position. I slept for two to three hours each evening—even on Secanol and other medication designed to knock me out. There was a huge pain under the skin in the back of my head above the paralyzed areas, but the medical staff, focused on my other physical problems, ignored my complaints. I guessed that the sore spot had to be auto glass. Every few days when someone gave me a bed bath, I'd ask if they could tend to the glass in my head. Nobody helped. I never even got my hair washed in the VA Hospital in Oklahoma City. It drove me nuts until after about a month, it festered and behold—out oozed a piece of windshield!

Steve Dicarlo was my primary physical therapist. He was a caring professional entertained by my stories of predicted recovery. With legitimate doubts and hopes, he ranged my arms, legs, hands and toes and graded for new movement. Muscles are graded on a five point system - 0 - no palpable tone, 1 - trace tone palpated, 2 - poor, with some distinct movement with gravity eliminated, 3 - fair, with some distinct movement against gravity, 4 - good, with movement against some resistance, 5 - normal. Steve palpated my muscles and encouraged me. "Hodge, I feel a trace left triceps!" His words were good news and I rejoiced.

When I told him that my hands burned more, Steve got excited and said, "That's a good pain and a sign of recovery."

My education was continuous.

Sensation is difficult to describe. Many receptor sites send signals to the brain. Made simple, they report light touch, deep touch, pain, temperature, vibration and other phenomena like identifying objects without looking at them. The sensory system has great bearing on movement. In clinical research, a scientist damages a cat's spinal cord by cutting the sensory nerves in the back of the cord known as the "dorsal column." They leave the motor nerves in the front intact. The research cat can't move after the refined injury due to sensory loss—even though the movement nerves are left intact.

My sensory testing could go from mundane to dramatic on any day. Steve would ask, "Which toe am I bending?"

I would say, "Right big one."

He would say, "Okay, you got that right three for three. Now which way am I bending it?"

I didn't know. I guessed, "Up." I was wrong.

Therapy began to be focused on regaining range and on developing neuromuscular strength. Later we progressed to attaining higher levels of coordinated activity, like balanced sitting and dressing. We take many abilities for granted—including physiological responses. These were painful to experience. Steve sometimes got into trouble for working too long with me. His superiors often scolded him and sent him off to take care of others. He taught my sister more ways to help me—and he was thankful for her help. Bev was always positive, always sure. She never gave up, even when I thought I might. That, I guess, is why her middle name is Faith.

The Way We Were

Barbara had to be going through hell, but she didn't say anything. She had depended on my significant physical ability before I was injured—and was attracted by it. My humor and animation seemed to lift her spirits. Barb was a great companion who had joined me in a spontaneous effort to quit running alone on the rough side of Oklahoma City. We met at a stereo sale. Music and the lake kept us happy. We partied hard and loved often. Neither of us had family money—and we spent what we earned. I missed her and spent a lot of time remembering our times together.

One time Barb and I went to see ZZ Top and Santana with other bands in an outdoor show in Tulsa. We could find no ice—and the 105-degree summer sun could bake your brain. No quick stops anywhere in Tulsa had any ice when we arrived. We ended up filling an ice chest with sixty pounds of shaved ice from the ice plant there. We had to park two miles from the arena. With a couple of dozen brews packed with other staples, the ice chest weighed seventy-five pounds. It was like an oversized brick and too heavy to tote. Barb could not carry one end, as she was a slight five-foot-two. I slung the ice chest on top of my shoulder and walked it in. We had a killer of a good time and passed the day away into darkness.

Barbara and I were both south-siders. Prior to my wreck, we had lived together for quite awhile and fell in love—in that order. Although we were not married, we had the ties that bind. We also realized the degree to which we were playing house, identifying together with Bob Seger's song, "Night Moves."

Although I deserved no credit for treating Barb well, I did better than anyone else she had hooked up with. I built up her confidence. She quit smoking and dressed up more after we met. Her folks had met when her dad was in the Army. None of us had much but we did have each other.

Barbara was great with little kids including her nephew, Cory. I observed her loving traits and knew she would be good with her children in the future, but I was afraid of that thought and didn't ponder it much until I was hospitalized. I protected her and ran from my ghosts. Barbie gave me all a loving woman could give to a man who had set up barriers. She could have used my accident as a good excuse to leave but she stayed. We were stubborn about not letting this tragedy break us apart.

My crash caused a temporary set back in my mind. I never asked Barbara what she thought. Since she was not quick to speak, I wondered. I was sorry for her to have had to endure the consequences of me being bashed against the concrete in October. Without ceremony one day at my hospital bedside, we exchanged rings. Barb deserved much more.

Occupational Therapy

An occupational therapist came by and hooked a cuff to my paralyzed left hand. The cuff had a pencil in it with the eraser down. While face down in the Stryker, I learned to let gravity assist the returning but minimal movement in my arms by sweeping the eraser back and forth on a specific area. A stand for magazines and other items placed at arm's reach under the Stryker frame allowed me to practice independent activities. My OT gave me a couple of ceramic ashtrays that I could paint on this stand, but after two, she told me I was painting more than they had budgeted for me. She placed strange spoons and forks in the cuff so I could learn to feed myself again—at least face down.

Funny, the OT never came back one day and I never knew her name. I learned to turn pages and read *National Geographic* all night long from cover to cover. I would read every word in the magazines, including the list of editors inside the left cover. I wished others had an idea of the amount of time I spent looking down in a Stryker frame. The cuff adaptations helped me with returned independence and dignity, as well as with strength and coordination. Since I needed no more than two to three hours of sleep per night, my sanity was still within reach.

The traction tongs that were screwed in my head stuck out to connect to the weights. I could not turn sideways. I had mirrors adapted above and below my bed that allowed me a periscope view to the side. They vibrated with every spasm or mini-adjustment that was made in the Stryker. My side view allowed me to see people when I talked to them and to watch TV—even though the screen print reflected backwards. With the exception of a few killer headaches that the vibrating mirrors caused, I began to feel much better as I headed towards the end of my multi-week Stryker frame lifestyle. I envisioned how comfortable I would be again, without screws in my head, to be able to see from side to side. I looked forward to my spinal fusion day. I would then be allowed to lie in a hospital bed—and to sit up again!

My own adaptation reached beyond the scope of occupational therapy. Keener each day at listening to what was happening around me, I tuned in and heard much that I would never have noticed before my accident. Although not able to see the hustle—bustle, my ears perked up to around the corner conversations, including heated debates among the staff about the correct way to disassemble and reassemble the Stryker frame without dropping me. I learned to listen to the parts coming apart or together—so that I could cue the untrained when they were doing it wrong.

The nurses also told tales of patient abuse. One specific nurse laughed about an event in which she broke an older veteran's leg in a transfer sequence. Since the patient was aphasic and unable to talk or communicate, management never discovered her abuse. What a real nice caregiver—a shark swimming around in the chum and eating whatever she wanted. I named her Nurse Abuse.

Living in Homer's Frame

After weeks, the calluses on my hands and feet peeled off. My nose bled all the time due to the dry air inside the ward. Vaseline was placed in my nostrils to combat the bleeding. I had to fight so many battles at once.

Sustained weight on my chin and forehead in the opening of the Stryker developed pressure blisters on both areas. Ooching my chin down and dropping it in front of the frame strap relieved pressure and avoided deeper sores on my face. The reposition gave me some relief, but it put my neck in a noose and left me vulnerable.

Daily, I listened to a nurse assistant as he came through the ward taking blood pressures. He sounded like a broken record as he called out the same words to everyone he approached. "Sarge, here to take your blood pressure." He never said anything else—even to the nurses who screamed orders to him.

He always rushed away to the next person, with the same "Sarge" line. I decided he might be retarded, as the nurses gave him very simple commands and he had limited duties. I tried talking to him, but he didn't respond and never made eye contact—not once for weeks. I nicknamed him Sarge AFL-CIO, because I could read those large letters on top of his name tag. I never knew most staff by name like him because they did not offer introductions and I could not read many name tags.

Each day the weight of traction slid me up in the Stryker frame. The few inches of traction rope hooked into my head shortened as I wiggled upward and soon reached a point that it didn't pull on the weights anymore—resulting in no neck traction. Staff would come by and tell me they were going to pull my feet and relocate me downward a few inches. When they pulled, the rope lengthened and the stack of weights provided traction again.

One morning, Sarge AFL-CIO reversed course back to me without speaking. He grabbed my feet and pulled them, sliding me towards the foot of the Stryker. Without warning, I didn't have time to return my chin above the frame strap. As Sarge AFL-CIO heaved on my legs, my chin grabbed the strap. My broken neck whiplashed backwards, jerking the rope hooked to the traction tongs. The force batted the stack of weights tied to the other end of the rope and they flew up in the air. Then gravity reversed the course of the weighted plates and they collided back down on each other with a loud "clang, clang, clang, clang" noise. They yanked my neck with each successive termination of flight.

I reviewed all of my limbs and systems to see if my hard-earned, slow recovery survived. I wiggled my jaw to see if the tong screws had been ripped out of my head, but they felt secure. People in the area were awed by the event. Sarge AFL-CIO scurried away to the next patient and said, "Sarge here to take your blood pressure," as if nothing had happened. The doctor was summoned, but I was not hurt—just scared.

Generate Income

That day, I had company that stunned me in a different way. Forms were placed below me. "Just put an X here, where it says signature," the man from the Social Security Office said.

"What do you need my signature for?"

"It takes time to process the Social Security Disability Insurance paperwork."

I didn't ask questions because the thought posed a moral dilemma. Above all else, we learned to work in the Wood clan. Working meant you possessed integrity. Now I could not lift a finger. My dad, a survivor of three strokes, was a small man who hated a handout. He had an eighth grade education. Dad quit school to support his family when the Great Depression hit. He never spoke a word about my grandparents who had passed before I was born. I once saw a picture of the whole barefoot, *Grapes of Wrath* bunch which let me know that my bloodline specialized in hard labor. Dad emphasized that a man had to earn his keep. I agreed. In high school, he and Uncle Virgil scheduled me seven days a week. I washed dishes in Virgil's Coffee Shop and stocked groceries in the Wood Brothers Market. We lived on a dirt road with no air conditioning—Virgil and I lived on one side of a small duplex and mom and dad on the other. Each night, Virgil and I soaked our feet together. Work was a Wood tradition. What was my destiny now that I couldn't earn a wage? A good man would not accept social security at the age of twenty-four.

Even in this paralyzed predicament, I couldn't tolerate not being able to work. The Bible says if you don't work, you don't eat. Getting a government entitlement was against the values of my upbringing. Somehow, I would get off disability income, but had no idea how.

Torture Time

Nurse Abuse was proud of her abusive ways. She wore a black wig one day and a white wig the next. She enjoyed power and I was afraid of her. Steve from the PT Department went to another hospital to locate some Spenco "bunny boots" designed to keep the skin sores on my heels from sloughing off. Steve gave me a directive not to lose the bunny boots, as there would be no more. Ordering through the VA system could take months. Nurse Abuse stepped into my curtained area one night. In the corner of my eye, I saw her throw my bunny boots across the floor.

I said, "Could you please put those bunny boots in my cabinet?"

Nurse Abuse responded viciously. She held the syringe like a knife and stabbed the needle into my thigh, looked me in the eye and said, "God damn you, don't try to tell me what to do!" Nurse Abuse was sick. This was not the last time I'd be her victim.

Any sense of normalcy was well received. My brother John came from Kansas City to visit and we watched the heavyweight title fight on TV. I watched through the mirror from my Stryker as the fight heated up through the stretch. My brother and I grew up watching the "Gillette Friday Night Fights" with dad on black and white TV. It felt like old times to be with him. Without tact, Nurse Abuse walked up, turned the TV off and announced that visiting hours were over. It was indecent. I was glad John no longer carried a switch blade knife. He would have cut her liver out.

My brother was pissed and let her know. John tried to negotiate with Nurse Abuse back near the nurse's station and I was concerned about their exchange of insults. He came back ready for a fistfight. I pleaded with him to forget about what had happened because I had no way to protect myself once he left. The nurses were in a shift change meeting as he exited. John walked in and said, "I just want to thank all of you THIS MUCH!" He shot them the finger. I was a marked man for brutal punishment after that.

Cada Coda

Late one night, Mr. Booker arrived. He was a middle-aged man who had suffered a stroke. They restrained him in a bed next to my Stryker so he wouldn't fall out. Once tied, they all left.

Booker was in my mirror view. Sad but comical, he struggled to escape and said over and over, "CADA CODA . . . CODA CADA . . . OKAY!"

Booker repeated these words, in a variety of sequences, cadences, tempos and octaves. He thought he was speaking normally but had a suspicion it wasn't right. Technically, he had expressive aphasia—he could not express himself but he could understand. Booker eyed me in my mirror and spoke with the biggest smile I had seen in awhile. He said, "CADA CODA?"

Chum Water

He looked to me for reassurance that he was making sense. I told him he wasn't making any.

He cried and recited gibberish all night. Before dawn he became animated, looked at me and said, "Cada Coda-Cada Coda-Cada Coda!" He fought the restraints and managed to get out over the handrails, but with a leg and arm still tied. His paralysis and lost awareness of one side of his body were obvious. As Booker managed an unsafe, standing posture, I realized why he scurried to escape. He urinated on the floor in the dark and it splashed into my area, under my face. He exhaled in relief, "Cada COOODA—Cada Coooooda."

I fed myself breakfast under the Stryker with the adapted utensils and thought of my basset hound, Walter. I recalled wrestling in the back yard after work. On those hot summer evenings, we split a six-pack of beer before going to race motocross. Walter snored under my parked car while I rode. I felt the motorcycle handlebars in my stout upper body, smelled the leather racing boot melting against the exhaust pipe and heard the two-stroke engine scream as the knobby tires dug up the dirt track.

Racing was over now, I realized. I wanted to see Walter—and cried into my adapted food bowl. Mike Kuns happened by and sat down on the floor, with his legs crossed Indian-style. His posture put him at my level. I wept heavily. His strong but pleasant voice emerged. "Having a tough day?"

"If everyone would just give me a chance," I declared.

Mike assured me he would give me all the chances I needed. He protected my heart.

Later, Booker had company and I watched through the mirror.

Mrs. Booker said, "Book, take your time. Where is the safe deposit box key?"

Booker formulated a confident, methodical answer and responded, "Cada Coda."

His wife could no longer take it and left the area. Two friends of Booker popped in and he smiled bigger. One said, "Booker, you look good—how's the food?"

With enthusiasm, Booker said, "Okay!"

The other visitor asked, "How are they treating you?"

He let go of another enthusiastic "OKAY!" The three black men had a hearty laugh, but the questions began to require more elaborate responses.

One visitor said, "Book, quit joking with your wife about the safe deposit box key. When will you quit teasing her?"

Looking serious and emphatic, Booker proclaimed, "CADA CODA, OKAY!" Booker asked a question. "Cada Coda Coda Cada, Coda Cada, CODA CADA—Okay?"

The three stood sad and speechless. I laughed. Everything anymore seemed humorous.

Hired Help Could Kill You

My brother put the fear of God into me because I didn't know if Dr. Schoenhals was a board certified surgeon. John was sure he needed to be. I might forget to ask and John taped "Board Certified" on a piece of paper above me on the Stryker.

Later Dr. Schoenhals appeared. He described how he would perform a front fusion of my neck vertebrae, by dissecting through the skin and musculature. He planned to cut a dowel rod-sized hole in my vertebrae and place in the same-sized bone dowel graft taken from my hipbone. Bone chips would seal the fused area, tools would be removed, he'd sew me up and the two fused vertebrae would heal and be stronger than those above or below.

Shell shocked from all that had happened, his description seemed unreal. I trusted him but asked, "Are you board certified?"

"No."

I paled.

He gave assurances that I wouldn't be hurt.

I consented to put my X on the papers that someone would bring. Before he left, a pressing question on my mind reached my tongue. I asked, "What are my chances to walk again?"

"You don't have any chances. You can hope and you can pray." After a brief pause, he closed. "You will be scheduled within the next couple of days for surgery."

Nurse Abuse had a black companion whom I nicknamed "Nurse Assistant Slurspeech." Assistant Slurspeech loved to laugh at Booker and mimic him. She had a sense of humor, but with a mean streak. She was on drugs. Her speech was slurred and she acted like she was on "Queer Street." I had been around so long that nurses would come to me to talk about the others.

One evening, Nurse Assistant Slurspeech showed up acting mean. I was due for catheterization and to be turned face down until the middle of the night. My schedule meant I would be face down again before daylight. I requested a modified turning schedule that would allow me to be face up to see the sunrise. Nurse Assistant Slurspeech got in a demonic-like state. She left, came back and pulled the curtain closed. Alone in the darkness she said, "This is what you need." She held a dry catheter in my face, her eyes bulging with anger. Catheters have to have a lubricant to progress through the penis into the bladder, but this one had no lubricant. She repositioned and jammed it into me. The sensory recovery of my right side, including the inside of my penis, had become hypersensitive over time and I had right-sided hyper-reflexes. The catheter plunge caused enormous spasms. The searing pain intensified. I could not stop her nor protect myself from the abuse. She pumped the bulb up that anchored the catheter in me and I screamed. Slurspeech turned me face down in the Stryker, being certain not to interact. Before leaving, she looked under at me and said, "Now let's see how that makes you feel."

I awoke to the night shift nurse's startled voice. My eyes opened as she turned on the light. I was sweating profusely. Did a beach ball get placed underneath me? Weakness overtook my body. Something flowing across the floor caught my eye—my blood. My nurse assistant was scared and moved quickly. She turned me face up in the Stryker and irrigated my catheter. It had not been flowing. Surspeech had placed the catheter in my urethra shallow of my bladder and ballooned it open. The urethra was far too small for this. The balloon damaged the tissue and closed off all flow. My assistant began to cry. Alarmed, I watched the blood pouring from my penis. She worked to release urine from my bladder. I felt like I had been hit in the head with a ball bat. She irrigated my bladder and commented that way too much had drained out. The beach ball subsided. I was feverish. I wanted to sleep and was not with it. Staff started IV's and transferred me to ICU.

The ICU staff suctioned blue cheesey-looking matter out of my bladder through my penis. The pain was unbearable. I couldn't remember much but I knew that the staff on Ward 7 North intended to cause my bladder infection. For the next few days, I flinched each time someone suctioned the blue cheese—and dreaded my return to Ward 7 North.

Right before Veterans Day, they said I was to be transferred back to the torture chamber. By then my veins had collapsed from all the needles and they were shooting drugs into the back of my hands. I arrived late on 7 North and had a visit from a tearful nurse assistant. She was sorry and could lose her job by telling me that what had happened before being transferred to ICU was a planned event. The dry catheter had been "doctored up." She said, "Promise not to tell." I was gutted.

Machismo Act

I awoke on Veterans Day suspecting that I had died and gone to heaven. I smelled perfume, heard a commotion at my bedside and had a sensuous, visual male experience. Life was a cakewalk and there wasn't a worry. I smiled at three females and said, "Good morning! Who are you?"

Taken by the screws in my head but impressed with my machismo act, the three visitors leaned over me and smiled. They joined together, "Good morning!"

They were holiday visitors. What perfect timing. Each beauty queen had a colorful pageant ribbon wrapped around her. Sporting a cowboy hat in red was Miss Rodeo Oklahoma. Miss Indian America was quiet, but attractive. Miss Fort Gibson was tall and model thin. I didn't mind if they stayed forever.

The public relations person asked, "Can I take a picture?"

That week my friend Steve Vandemeer came by with the picture of the girls and me in the newspaper. The shot was placed in honor of Veterans Day. Steve and I laughed at the caption below the picture—I had the wrong name, Wilson. We guessed a Wilson got my suppository that day. I cherished the picture.

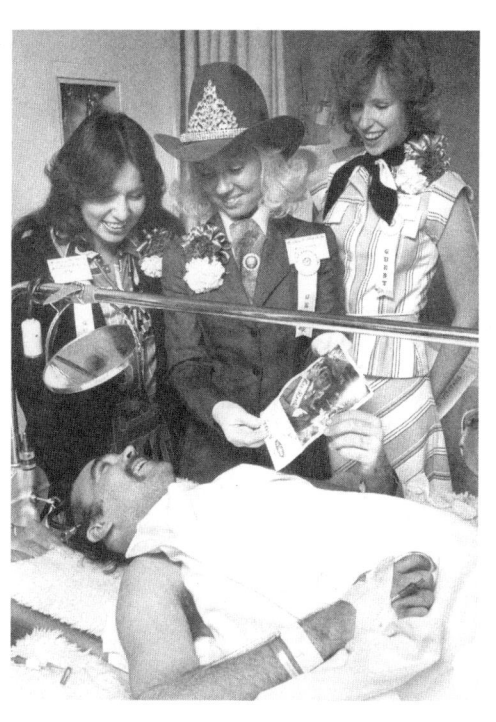

Dream to Walk, Live to Bleed

My best friend Michael P came by. We always called him Michael P. He was a humorous fellow with a rough exterior that covered a heart of gold. He used to tuck thick brown hair under a wig to attend Army reserve meetings, where he served as a Drill

Sergeant. Michael P had Indian blood and a Harley Davidson. We lived together for a while and were like brothers. The epitome of "Cool," Michael P lit the place up with street-learned, captioned comments about life. His visits were hard on him because he never expected to see my ass-kicking body stretched out paralyzed. He tended to get quiet by nature and that was never easy for me and certainly not now. Since we did everything together except commit murder, we managed our hospital dilemma like it was a jail visit. He made me more comfortable than anybody alive. We talked awhile and my spirit led me to confide a deep-rooted thought. "Michael P," I said. "I'm gonna walk out of this hospital."

Taken by the comment, he reflected back after a second. "Yeah, man, I believe you." He meant it—and so did I.

It was odd that I said this. I hadn't sat up for two months and they told my family to plan a nursing home placement with twenty-four hour care. A friend's mother continued to call prayer meetings for me. Whatever my fate, I had faith that Jesus would stay with me.

Staff members scurrying to complete tasks came to my Stryker frame to turn me. A quick spin was required to roll me over face up. While the spin was being made, I realized the two IV bags weren't moved first to the other side of the Stryker. The IV lines tightened up from the bags on the bottle stand and yanked hard. The needles in the back of my hands ripped out. Blood spurted.

The staff members got upset with each other, placed blame— and launched into a heated interaction. No one said anything to me. I was an object like a lamp on a table. They argued as if someone tripped over the electric cord and knocked the lamp over. Who would talk or apologize to a lamp?

A nurse re-inserted the IV's. She didn't speak. I initiated my four-hour, face-up time deep in thought. I had learned what to say —nothing. Being quiet was hard on a working man who once brought the fight and thought he could never be beaten.

Chum Water

Own Football Stadium

Barb and my family joined me on the ward while I got my preoperative shots for spinal surgery. I wanted to get out of the Stryker and traction. However, what I KNEW was coming next preoccupied me. I wondered if they would use enough anesthetic to put me to sleep before the surgery began. My fear was understandable with the way things had gone. I was like a dog on a short chain being beaten on a regular basis. I imagined the club was going to fall again soon but I didn't know why and could not get away.

I was obsessed with the thought of getting carved on through the front of my neck and feeling the knife cut me. I had made a point of not getting stabbed in life, although the opportunity arose. I recalled the multiple steps necessary to go into my neck that Dr. Schoenhals had described. Like a magician in Vegas, my mind played tricks on me. Getting opened up while not being able to say or do anything was horrifying. The reality of dying occurred to me, but I shelved that worry knowing that if it happened, the next stop was favorable. It's just that I preferred to be knocked out as cold as a block of ice before getting cut on.

I had nothing to worry about. They rolled me into the ice-cold surgery room where everything was green or silver. Huge lights faced down as if I had my own personal football stadium. There was one seat on the fifty-yard line and I was in it lying in the center of the huddle. When they put the sodium pentothal in my vein, I planned to count all the way down from one hundred and then request another dose. I never started the count.

A strange, spirit based dream hit me while the doctors fused my neck. An air-powered tire wrench took the Stryker from my traction and weights—sounding like lug nuts being removed. God grabbed me by the hardware in my head and threw me across the ocean. Free and flying like a glider, I landed and sank to the bottom of the sea. Still paralyzed, the weight from my tractional tongs anchored me in the current. I began to drown and God said, "Go worship me." He took me by the leg and swept me into the air above the water. It was a sensational hallucination.

I awoke and realized that the surgery was over because they were unscrewing the tongs from my head. They came out quicker than they had gone in. Feeling like getting teeth pulled, the screws made a loud noise as they came loose from my skull. I was happy they were coming out, not in. I conversed with the man who had placed me in a SOMI neck brace.

"I made it?" I asked. My tongue felt like a stick in my mouth. The surgery drugs had dried up all secretions.

"You can't be awake yet," he responded while applying the brace.

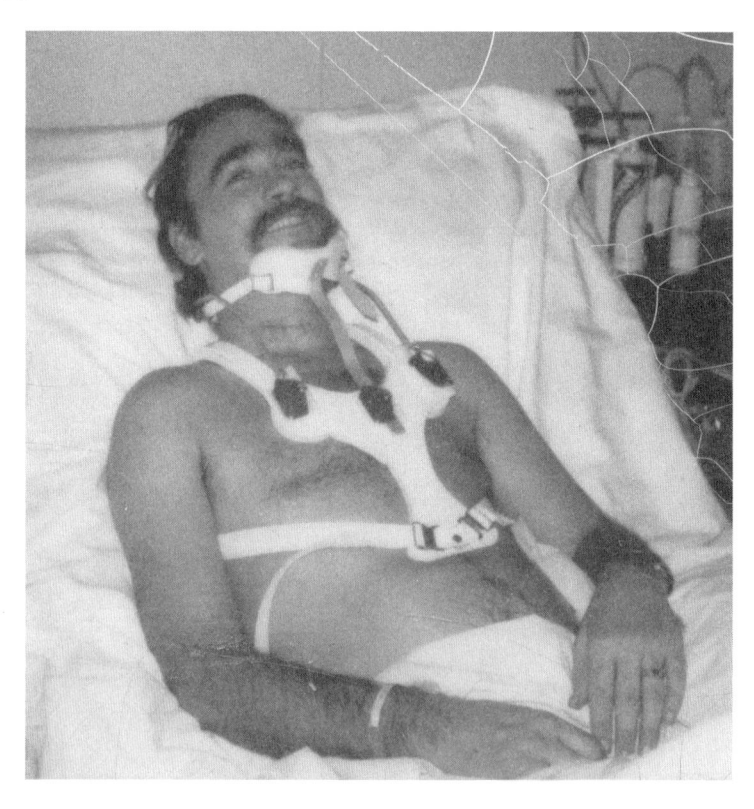

"Am I in the recovery room?"

"Yes, but it's too early. You can't be awake yet."

That was good enough for me. I pondered the dream—and looked to the future.

A Piece of Cake

I went to the ICU to stabilize and they said I could try sitting up. I was ready to wheel a chair around for a little while, walk and go home. I said, "A piece of cake—can't wait." I knew it would be easy.

When they sat me up in bed, I knew that it was a mistake—my head felt like it might blow apart and I thought I would faint. Once the body gets used to not being up it makes many physiological adjustments. My system had grown unaccustomed to sitting upright. I was short of breath. I felt like I would fall out of bed and had no way to catch myself. Things were ninty degrees out of phase—everyone walked on the walls in my mind's adjusted eye. Clammy and dizzy, I pleaded, "Lay me out flat again."

Exhausted and exasperated with not being able to tolerate sitting, I tried to sleep. The bed was like lying in a pile of marshmallows. I couldn't make the smallest adjustment. Though wrong, I was certain it wasn't me. Fighting gravity to feed myself was a losing battle. My mother fed me and I was discouraged.

I looked at Mom's wrinkled face and hands. Her hair was gray but she had an air about her that everyone enjoyed. She put beauty in ugly places. It was sad she worked on her feet all day in a bakery and then fed me before going home to take care of dad. Mom was skinny in her sixty-sixth year. She smoked too many cigarettes and had since she was nine. I said, "Mom, sorry you have to feed me."

Mom smiled and her reassuring but tired eyes matched her smile. "Hodge, I fed you when you were a baby and I'm glad to do it again."

Her comment made me mad but I said nothing else before she went home.

Steve from physical therapy came by and identified the goals of therapy included regaining bed mobility, sitting tolerance, feeding while sitting, transferring and propelling a wheelchair. I accepted the reality of my situation but it hit hard and humbled me.

Going back to the same ward scared me, but that was the next destination. The doctor ordered a special bed cushion to protect my skin. Steve educated me about the cushion and emphasized bedsores could delay or destroy recovery efforts. "Be sure to get someone to plug the cushion in on 7 North," he said before leaving.

Back in 7 North, nobody responded to my request to plug the cushion in to save my skin. Left to lie there, worry and pray for mercy, the Lord comforted me. Skin sores developed and their scars remain. Nothing was ever a piece of cake after my accident.

Level Playing Field

As a habit, the nursing staff took me to therapy late and sent me soiled. Bowel and bladder problems follow spinal injury, along with dozens of other issues. It would be better to minimize the effects of all the new problems by providing caring services, but that wasn't the case. I wanted every minute available in therapy and shortening my assigned time added to the frustration. The staff used a tilt table in PT to raise me up on my feet while monitoring my blood pressure. The goal was "safe tolerance, 90 degrees." As they strapped me to the table, I asked Steve if he was sure that I wouldn't fall out. He rolled the table toward upright and I felt as compressed as concrete. "Jeez." The crushing effects of gravity made me short of breath.

Steve said, "Blood pressure is going down—get him down."

They hurried to get me flat.

We tried again.

"I can't take it," I said after a few seconds. "Get me down."

We kept trying each day and timed my tolerance. I rose up and my lungs hardened. There were reasons for this. Sitting and standing are abrupt motions and physiological challenges. Each session left me demolished. It was hard work, but my physiology slowly adjusted and eventually, I reached the goal. I could sit up again without passing out.

With my boxing, football, motocross, wrestling, fist fighting and manual labor background considered, I had the "suck-em-up" spirit of a warrior—but nothing came easy in my new circumstances. At first, I couldn't roll over to my side from my back. We tried each day. I could propel a wheelchair a short distance with a chest strap to keep from falling. If I slipped too far off center, someone had to reposition me. A ton of help was required to transfer me to a wheelchair and I didn't have the trunk balance to sit on a treatment mat. In due time, I fed myself with adaptations in bed after learning to hook my wrist under a bed rail and coming up on my left elbow. As my endurance improved, I tolerated longer sitting periods.

As we achieved the prescribed goals and I grew stronger, motion in my left arm and hand began returning. I had a fair left thigh muscle and the back of my leg contracted. My right side was not as good and it shrunk up. I hated to look at my right arm and leg—and could not believe they were mine. The bulging right triceps I admired in the mirror the night I walked out of my home couldn't even be felt.

Bobby, my other PT, propped my right knee up on a coffee can each day. She barked signals to kick and elevate my foot. She felt for a muscle contraction. Then one day my foot moved! Bobby screamed at Steve, "He's got a right quad—he's got a right quad!"

They rolled me to eliminate gravity and we tried the right quad again. It was miraculous. I moved a new muscle group after nothing for weeks. We celebrated and I progressed further.

Steve asked me one day if I wanted to stand up and walk.

"Sure ... How?"

"In the parallel bars—we will help." We talked through the sequence and set short goals.

Days later, I stood with help and then one day it was time to step. I stood and looked down the bars like a gymnast, concentrating on perfect technique. After a zillion tries with leg braces on and staff lifting and placing my feet, I walked between the bars. Someone trailed me with a wheelchair until I dropped back in it—exhausted and exhilarated. The time up was brief and beautiful.

Now I was back to a level playing field. Mike Kuns arranged my transfer.

I had a plane to catch.

Flying First Class

The transfer excited me. The medical staff rolled me on the stretcher to the ambulance. I gagged on the smell of raw gasoline. I asked where the spill was.

They responded, "What gas?"

There were no normal city odors inside the hospital. Now my nose seemed stuck in a gasoline can. After so many physical losses, I loved having a nose like a bird dog. Likewise, the screeching of tires and hum of traffic were intense. After weeks of indoor confinement, I had developed ears like a deer. To be outside again thrilled me. My new senses were entertaining—and flying fit into my schedule. The ambulance headed for a small airport. I never had a clue where it was located.

On the tarmac, I suspected that a baggage handler discussed with the ambulance crew the whereabouts of my luggage. I knew that this would be a short discussion since I had no clothes on, hadn't had any on since they cut them off the night of my wreck in

Chum Water

October — and had no luggage. I watched the baggage handler sign papers and get in the cockpit of a one-prop plane and I realized that he was the pilot, not the baggage handler. The transport staff slid me on the gurney into the plane headfirst on my back under the pilot's elbow. They placed a blanket on me and shut the door.

The pilot asked, "Are you ready?"

"Yes, sir."

We taxied and took off. I looked at the dash wiring below the pilot's elbow and enjoyed the flight.

We landed in Memphis, Tennessee.

Spare Parts

The ambulance crew pushed my stretcher through the Veterans Spinal Cord Injury Center to the fifth floor nursing station. I sensed a change in atmosphere. This staff acted happy. Most were black folks. I felt no tension like on Ward 7 North. Everyone spoke with southern accents that were hard to understand. The reception was warm and I needed that.

The same dull decor surrounded me, but things were cleaner and certainly more pleasant. One exception was a faint but distinct, pungent smell. Placed in a room with three others, I noted that the smell lingered. My new roommates told me that the funk was from skin sores. Men who had open skin sores that exposed their bony areas filled the fourth floor. These lesions challenged survival and many died. Veterans battled skin sores on my floor, too. The smell of rotten flesh permeated our areas. Both floors housed the paralyzed and patients for the most part were bedridden. I got used to the smell but I never got used to the pile of human debris.

A young roommate received a gunshot in the neck that had splintered his spinal cord. He lost control from the neck down. His shoulders fell out of their sockets if they weren't supported in arm troughs. He had a mouth control to call attendants and make minor adjustments on the TV and radio. However, the slug took his voice. He didn't have much to say anyway and stared into the distance. The respirator did the breathing. He lived for nothing.

Residents didn't know each other well. They housed their pain. In therapy, we stayed busy. Meals came to our rooms. The injured made no door-to-door visits. The staff kept everyone up to date on each newcomer's horrible fate. Men dove into rocks, got crushed, blown up, shot, electrocuted, beaten, or maimed. It was overwhelming so you faced your own problems and attended a bingo game or social event if you were well enough. A urine bag hung on your wheelchair handlebar. Everybody wore the same brown paper bag-colored shirts labeled VA HOSPITAL. Nothing else could be done with us, so here we stayed. Pieces remained of each person housed in the Spinal Center. It was a human warehouse of spare parts. Nobody exchanged addresses for the future. You shipped out to use what worked.

Bowel Training Class

The doctor saw me for evaluation and processing. He said to attend bowel-training class. I preferred not to enroll but nobody asked my opinion. After spinal injury, functions taken for granted don't work. You lack the normal urge to go to the bathroom or it's too late to react when you get the signal to go. The circuits get confused, the spinal injured body reacts and the person with a cord injury deals with it for the rest of life. The experience is more fun than getting beaten with a nightstick.

One of four specific actions happens after you ding your cord and need to squat. (1) A roll of the dice determines whether your spastic system throws or holds poop. (2) Nothing happens and your body launches into overload with life threatening consequences. (3) You go all the time—anywhere and everywhere. Nothing enhances sex life less. (4) Someone stuffs medicine or fingers in your rump to elicit an outcome.

Nobody taught me any of this in bowel training class, but I did learn about the health care system's dark side—and a rude awakening lay ahead. None of my roommates said anything about bowel training class before we left. Everyone kept their heads down and I wondered what was up. My attendant placed me naked on a rolling bedside commode. He wrapped a blanket around me, propped me so I wouldn't fall out of the chair and pushed me down the hall and into a large bathroom. He locked the brakes and I faced half of the unit residents who were placed in a circle. They were all draped like me. Male and female attendants wore rubber gloves and scurried to place large, silver bowls underneath each of us. They passed out "silver bullets," their term for laxative suppositories, and made light of the situation.

"A shitty job," they said.

Like a well-executed football play, the attending staff placed the suppositories in a well-timed sequence that allowed them to run. A command cleared the room. "The fuse is lit! Quick, get outta here before they shit!"

One attendant stayed to monitor the "class." We looked distant and said nothing. Within twenty minutes, bombs away. A pitiful odor that might make your teeth turn green hung like fog in the air. We tried not to look at each other. Once the chemical worked, the attending staff returned. If someone's bowels didn't move, a staff member used fingers.

Gary yelled out his favorite line. "Just diggin' shit—I just don't know how long I can keep diggin' shit."

They retrieved and dumped the silver bowls. Bowel movement defined the order as we were lined up in a column for a shower. An attendant removed my blanket and exposed me like the rest. Indwelling catheters protruded and filled leg bags. Staff at the shower entry applied a lather of soap upon us and scrubbed. We waited in line for the rinse where a female handled the spray hose. She wore a swim cap and a white, waterproof apron like a butcher. Once rinsed, someone threw a towel on me and took me back to the room. Bowel training class was over for the evening.

My class met every other weeknight. The other half of the residents went on the opposite nights. Using this method, our bowels moved in assembly line fashion followed by a shower. Unless you went elsewhere, the bowel learned a regular schedule —in objective theory. Reality, over theory, became clear—there were limited staff available to complete the task at hand. How convenient. This defecating experience felt most indecent and removed our dignity.

Cowboys on the Cattle Drive

I lost track of sequence, became tenacious about my therapy — and slogged through my past. My harsh reality denied insightful thoughts about the future. I searched my soul for answers but there were none. Minutes turned into weeks. What did I do wrong in life to deserve such a fate? I forgot that I was a pretty good Joe. As the past and present melted together, I let go of my old self and met the new one to find an identity. That search continued.

What happened first and next was gone. Chronology and dates became unclear from December until I got out of the hospital in March. My mental processing shut down each evening and turned back on the next morning to start the routine anew.

After not wearing clothes for over two months, they began dressing me and it felt like I was wearing a sandpaper suit and wooden blocks for shoes. The body adjusts to sensory input and without that input, it becomes hypersensitive. I trained to be left-handed since my right side prognosis was poor. In occupational therapy, I followed a slow and tedious process of development. My teeth substituted for my right hand. Buttons and zippers required adaptive aids. Shoes tightened with elastic laces.

Phylisine was my PT. She stretched me out in blood-curdling fashion. Every task required concentration. Although several were conquered, the degree of difficulty went off the chart. Phylisine taught me how to roll over to my stomach and then to rise up on my knees and hands. Later I stood in parallel bars without support.

Phylisine helped me become capable of getting to the bed, toilet and shower by myself. Weights further strengthened my muscles. These therapies made two-a-day football practice look like a picnic. It was tedious but over months, my independence returned.

A rugged path of improvement led to the ability to put on a few clothes again. Sweat pants and pullover shirts, like my brown bag-colored VA prisoner attire, didn't have buttons or zippers. I wore slip on shoes and wheeled to the gift shop and cafeteria. The Corrective Therapy Department made arrangements for me to workout in addition to my regular schedule of appointments. In these special sessions, pulleys were available for wheelchair exercise and I could stand alone in parallel bars. Burning pain in my arms and legs and below my chest accompanied my physical progress every instant of the day and night. Despite these problems, I felt lucky to be doing so well.

On trips to the john, I wiped left-handed with numb, slow fingers and weak trunk muscles. Frustrated, I wished others might switch hands and try wiping their buns to get a partial picture. It got worse. Bowel accidents were normal and they tore me up.

I was down the hall from my room, tired and spastic from working so hard. My body signaled an emergency and bowel movement process number one for a person with spinal injury reared its head. With no warning, nature took over.

"No, no, not this again. Get there Hodge—wheel this damned thing!" I muttered in a panic.

I pushed the wheelchair, determined to speed up but unable to go fast. I reached the bathroom. I rose up, balanced against the toilet safety bars and lowered my pants down—a difficult challenge even when not rushed. At the same time, Mother Nature finished her process and poop flew down my legs, into my pants and shoes and onto the raised toilet seat, porcelain and floor. I needed more balance and coordination to clean up alone. I leaned over the toilet bar and surveyed my predicament.

"Real damned nice," I said to myself.

This was neither the first nor the last time to shit all over myself. I hated to ask for help and wished for a gun so that I could make it the last time. Humiliated, I pulled the cord on the wall for assistance and began to field clean my mess.

Buck from Georgia broke his neck diving. A bona fide rebel, he tattooed his name across the back of his four knuckles on each hand. Although he no longer had grasp, Buck held his arm up, imitated a fist and tried to feign throwing it at me. As he pretended, he chuckled and said, "Here, eat this and read that Buck hit ya." Buck's wife and baby came to visit from time to time. They had a long way to go to find a way to make it.

I met a man lying on a gurney. He aired out his butt to heal open skin sores. This healing lasted months sometimes and we took the time to shoot the bull. He told me of a time when he was in traction. A doctor turned to leave and caught the traction weights in his lab coat pocket. Doc didn't realize he was hung up in the weights. The screwed in tongs ripped from his head. I doubted the experience added to the doctor's reputation for good bedside manners. The story took my breath, for sure.

Mr. Cole had a flat-top haircut and a flat-topped head. Cole scared people and we avoided him like the plague, except to gang up with verbal abuse. He wore the same funky T-shirt every day. Able to bathe without help, Cole didn't. His body odor collapsed lungs. Cole thought he was Romeo around women. Otherwise, he hated everybody and everything. He disliked black people and said rude things to our attendants. Cole faked most of his injury. When he walked behind the knee-high curtain, his feet moved normally. If a staff member headed his way, Cole became gimpy and put on his soft neck collar. I figured him for a sick puppy. I noticed Cole got up behind the curtain and walked to a spot, stood there awhile and went to lie back down quite often. One day the curtain was pulled open and Cole had a pint of whiskey in a flowerpot on the ledge. He was discharged later. No one mourned.

Joe was a respected man, not an outlaw like most of us. Middle-aged and older than the rest, his caring wife and beautiful children moved to Memphis to stay close to him. With a lifetime of honorable service in the the Air Force and retirement close at hand, Joe got hung up in some high wires. Electricity entered his lower body and blew his head apart. It reformed his skull and created a mountain peak out of the top of it. The current tried to suck his brain up and out of his brain box. It even blasted his eye orbits out of alignment. Joe couldn't close his mouth so he drooled and spoke slowly. He wore a helmet and was paralyzed. Everyone said it was a miracle that Joe had lived. I could not help but ponder why God didn't take him. Praying for miracles, Joe and his wife chain-smoked cigarettes in the hall. OT issued him a holding cuff with a clip so that she could place a smoke in his hand and light it. These nice people had a mean future.

Heartfelt arguments broke out between the paralyzed who couldn't get out of bed. Fights guaranteed violence. "I'm gonna come over there and whoop your ass as soon as I am able," they would say. The "Freshly Maimed Comedy Club" provided odd entertainment.

I possessed a lot of pent-up aggression. Two of us on the fifth floor eventually were able to walk again. The other veteran was an Army captain and chaplain serving in Germany until a trooper rolled a jeep and broke his neck. By chance and not choice, I found myself captured in his audience. He demanded attention and asked for too much help and it grated on me. Right or wrong—I didn't think he worked to get better. We were an odd couple. I nicknamed him Chaplain Gimpy.

Chaplain Gimpy asked his wife to do everything. She moved to Memphis and assumed the role of slave—and the catering made my butt suck mud. Both of us knew our injuries tarnished our faith. It was unfair of me early in his recovery, but I expected spiritual leadership from him. He bitched and moaned. I worked hard not to slap Chaplain Gimpy around.

Chaplain Gimpy said, "I am not certain Jesus is real. Why would he let me get hurt like this?"

Chaplain's uncertainty upset me. "I am sure of my faith," I said—and then had doubts too.

I begged him to quit blaming God. Chaplain Gimpy went on and on in self-pity, voicing anger at Christ. In response to his doubts about God and slanting in on his chaplain status, I had had my fill. It proved that I, too, lacked Christian-centered behavior. I said, "You know you're off work. Are you going to stay clocked out, you pathetic S.O.B.?"

One day Chaplain Gimpy's behavior gnawed on me too much. I lost all signs of grace and shot him the finger using the famous four-letter word that could get your teeth knocked out in most social settings. Life can be confusing. The Good Book could have refreshed our memory that we are all special to God, but cowboys on the trail don't feel special and our memories were stale.

A Fish Returns to Water

Phylisine placed me in aquatic therapy. She advised me to be ready for a challenge. "Don't worry," she said. "The staff will hold you above water."

Her caution made my tail feathers spread like a spring Tom turkey. I chimed back, glowing with confidence. "Jeez—can we go now?" Phylisine listened to me boast about how well I could swim and ski. It was a lengthy presentation that gave her an earful about my summer devotion to water worship. I could not wait to get in the pool.

That night I dozed off and had a vision. I stood in the lake water as Barbara, on the bank and in the bright moonlight, slipped off her bikini. She ran naked and my brain took arousing snapshots of her petite body. We skinny-dipped in shoulder-deep water. She wrapped her legs around me and I grasped each side of her tight bottom and lifted her from the lake floor and held her against me.

We kissed and her big brown eyes revealed I had reached her most erotic senses.

The light to my hospital room switched on and I jumped.

"Time to drain your catheter bag," said the attendant.

After he left, I knew it was a matter of time before Barb and I would again be having orgasmic sex—and I dozed back off.

The next morning I was ready to swim but the nurse came in with another plan. She asked, "Want to try an intermittent catheterization program?" She told me I had to drink fluids and pee off all but a small amount of residual urine. They would catheterize me each time to measure what remained. If I made the grade I could use an external catheter. I did not want an indweller. I thought about the new possibilities.

Without emptying the bladder you will croak—or get sick enough that you will wish to croak. I already had infections that had come close to killing me. The staff said that drinking lots of cranberry juice decreased infections. I drank gallons and would have sucked out the sewer line if it would have helped me heal. That's all they taught in the hospital—drink cranberry juice. Later, I learned much more. The bladder has two muscles that work together to release urine. Their action is much like a balloon blown up, with the hole crimped closed to hold the air in and released to let the air out. This action goes spastic after spinal injury. Pee problems arise like a car that's had its spark plugs rearranged. The muscles malfunction and fire at the same time—or not at all. Soon, all else fails. If you keep an indwelling catheter in all the time, the clock is ticking on getting ill or dying due to infection. Like bull riders, it's not if, but when and how bad.

For me, progression to an external was not a simple no-brainer. I could feel the tube go in now. Slurspeech's abuse caused mental scars. Staff style and skill varied and I wondered who picked their butt before inserting the hose into my sacred zone. I figured that now they planned to do it more often. My brain boxed the experiences up, realized the dangers and told me to be scared. However, I decided to take the pain and counseled my brain to believe me.

I was determined not to fail the test. If I needed someone to jump up and down on my stomach to make the grade that the nurse described, then on my back I'd go and they could stomp on me. The pee would squash out before she measured it. Exploratory drilling started and soon I got rid of the indweller.

In my small mind, I imagined myself hanging it out, relaxing, releasing a stream and then flushing the toilet. That was dead wrong. I never knew when I would jettison fuel. Of all the problems with spinal injury, bowel and bladder control headed the list. Later, anytime I walked into a store, mall, or formal function, I introduced myself by saying, "Hi, I'm Hodge. Where's the restroom?" I was lucky that I enjoyed the outdoors.

Finally, my scheduled pool time arrived. It hit me that I LOVED the water and was going back in! God punched my fun ticket for admission as an attendant rolled my wheelchair near the pleasure pond. The humid air filled my lungs and was nothing less than delightful. I enjoyed the echo sounds that bounced from the water's surface into the tile walls. I hoped that maybe they would just leave me all afternoon, everyday in the pool! They pushed me next to the edge of the pool. I smiled at my reflection. Soon I would stand up and relax on the bottom tiles. I imagined cool air bubbles trickling against me to the surface and relieving my burning pain. The water would be easy to move in, once buoyancy equalized my weight. Heaven was a foot or two away and I was to be admitted.

Thoughts raced through my head about returning to water. I couldn't believe they thought I'd need help. Why didn't they enroll me in the pool program earlier? Staff embarrassment would be understandable once they saw how I could swim. I rehearsed accepting their apologies. Just throwing me in would be fine. They didn't know any better. Eager to enter, my first move would be a quick spin to my back, followed by a strong stroke to impress everyone. With water dancing along the edge of my face, I'd float with ease, supported by my venue of freedom. The fish returns.

    They rolled me down the ramp and the unseen currents threw me out of the seat. The water caused me to burn more and elicited spasms. To my surprise, I went face down and thumped my cheek against the side of the pool. Submerged and eyeballing the edge, I reached for it but missed. I breathed water and had not prepared for that. My lungs were weak and could not expel the chlorinated moisture and it stung my insides. The water bounced me back and forth like a towel in a washer, out of control. Passing wall tiles and watching them one by one, I strained to right myself. I kicked but failed to stand. In doing so, the top of my left toes scraped on the rough bottom tiles. I had no water skills. The staff held me up and laughed. My perceptions had never been so wrong. Thankful they brought me up, I saw no humor. Clinging to the side of the pool and supported by others, a five-day per week struggle began in aquatic therapy with hopes of someday enjoying the water. This fish returned to his preferable place but he could not swim.

Three ~ Stink Bait

Outside the Bars

I advanced to a hard collar from the rigid neck brace and figured to wear a soft collar soon. Phylisine put a posterior leaf in my tennis shoe to control my foot drop. She said that if I were to be able to walk again, I would need a hinged Ankle Foot Orthosis. Each day and for weeks in the parallel bars, Phylisine helped my right leg go forth on each step.

I inched forward and gained confidence that I would walk. Traversing within the bars, I thought of many things at once. My left leg was getting stronger—but it remained numb as if anesthetized—and I had to visualize where I had placed it. My right triceps, wrist and hand would not support me or break gravity and my right hand rolled up in a spastic pattern known as a synergy. My strong hand had numbness and loss of position sense. I had a Brown Sequard Syndrome—poor movement on one side and poor sensation on the other. I walked and spasms dumped me. The staff dared to help me recuperate and against predictions, I saw light at the end of the tunnel. I called Michael P and said that even though I didn't walk out of the first hospital, I would walk out of this one. He planned a trip to bring Barbara out. I imagined the look and feel—walking outside the parallel bars.

Football Mentality Meets Shrinker

We were required to attend the psychologist's sessions. Empathy was not a tool he used and the rules were slanted. Rule One: whatever this guy said was the gospel truth. Rule Two: if you planned to go anywhere or do anything while in captivity, you better voice support for Rule One.

The psychologist slapped group material together, stuck to a theme and delivered lines like he was reading from a book. "You will never again ejaculate or have orgasm," the Shrinker announced to the young men in wheelchairs circled for open forum. "Accept it." Some of the men were required to have their wives present. The Shrinker asked, "Who would like to comment?"

Jeez. I wouldn't want to comment to a group about that. Neither did anyone else. The Shrinker had us by the balls though. If we wanted to play bingo or go on an outing, we had to first acknowledge that we agreed with him. I took a moment and thought over what the Shrinker liked to talk about. It needed to be discussed in private. Okay, I can't move. Okay, I am going to crap all over myself. Okay, I will never pee right. Yes, teach me how to go on a job interview. Tell me how to explain how, once hired, there might be an occasional problem in that I might pack my pants and have to go home early. The psychology sessions were out of control. Did the Shrinker in these group interventions consider dignity? Did this group need to be gathered to hear me reflect on never busting my nuts again?

The Shrinker thought so. I tried to humor him and lighten the air by changing the subject from the group's apparent fate to never ejaculate. Forget it. Back to the theme—tell these strangers what you think about not ever achieving orgasm again. The Shrinker depressed all of us by the time the group finished. With a big smile, he then extended an invitation to go with him to see Gorgeous George wrestle the Great Bolo at the Memphis Coliseum.

"Hmmm," I thought. I hadn't been anywhere. Sounds like fun. "Can I go, please?"

He marked me down on the list. Then he blew me away and asked, "Do you like football?"

I ignited. "You bet'cha!"

Football taught me to get up when knocked down. I learned to play with pain. I served others on the football field. Fierce pride used in a noble way on the field made us winners. Football made players learn self-discipline, to give and take—and how small details make a difference. It seasoned me so I could enjoy challenges and remain positive in victory or defeat. It helped me survive a near fatal accident. I sacked groceries better, ran a sales route hard and in any weather and studied due to the game. Because football taught me to tackle things bigger than myself, I learned to finish the impossible. Even with the flu, I crawled through freezing water under the house, in the middle of the night during an ice storm, to fix a busted water line. Without football, I would not have done that.

I couldn't believe my ears. Shrinker would take us to the Liberty Bowl if we behaved. Members of this human warehouse of spare parts could choose to head outside of the walls and go see a college football game. Elvis Presley died in August and the dedicated halftime show in his hometown of Memphis would be a cherished, once-in-a-lifetime experience. Mr. Shrinker set up a wonderful excursion. In our group, he dictated the requirements.

Shrinker said, "I arranged for the Mothers of Deceased Vietnam Veterans to assist us by providing blankets that they have made for you," the Shrinker related. "These women will be going to the game with us on the hospital bus." He continued. "You guys will have to watch your language."

There was the damning statement that always rolled from Shrinker's tongue. Why did he say it? I guessed he feared we would talk about our mass murder experiences or bring up how a Bouncing Betty blew a buddy's balls off in Vietnam. Without prompts, I would treat these women with great respect. Why did Shrinker have a poor conception of us? He didn't know anyone. Why did he want complete mind control before we could be a part of things? Before I was hurt, I could have made Shrinker eat concrete for the things he said to me. I imagined how good it would feel to meet him on the wrestling mat, shake hands and wrestle. I would have worn him down for two periods then put him in a Guillotine pin hold until his ribs and neck ripped through his carcass from my stretch. But, hold on, I thought. The refreshing notion to take things out on Shrinker passed. Instead, I assured him that I wouldn't endanger the guests. After all—I would be going to a COLLEGE FOOTBALL GAME!

As bowl games approached, my wildest imagination had never pictured me attending one. Since a near fatal evening back in the fall, I had done no more than sit outside in a wheelchair. Yes, the Lord blessed me now because these eyes would see my beloved Oklahoma Sooner's Big Eight rival, Nebraska, play football. They would face the Atlantic Coast Conference Champions, North Carolina. This would be the Tar Heels first meeting with the Cornhuskers from the Big Eight. I had one thought etched inside my brain—set up the line of scrimmage!

In Oklahoma and Nebraska, we were used to being National Champions. The Sooners were Champs in '74 and '75 and the Cornhuskers in '70 and '71. Both programs finished in the Top Ten every year during the seventies, except for Nebraska this season. They lost to the Sooners in the conference shootout. North Carolina had a lot to prove in beating Nebraska and the Tar Heels were favored to win. They had stars, including a freshman and future Hall of Famer named Lawrence Taylor, who wouldn't even play.

I predicted Nebraska would win and voiced my opinion to Mr. Shrinker. He didn't like it. Someone said he graduated from North Carolina, where he got his "Masters of Shrinking Degree" that his mother paid for. His impression that I had shit for brains was just dandy going into the football game. He couldn't manipulate what was to happen on the football field and my intellect would gain his reconsideration as we watched the Cornhuskers hammer his Alma Mater. How perfect.

Heading towards game day, I held my hat in my hand when talking to Shrinker and made certain to use manners so as not to be left out. Hopefully, we would sit side by side during the contest. Cheering at a football game came natural and my lungs would roar for his benefit. I listened to him leading up to the game. He adored his North Carolina team. Mr. Shrinker could say what he wanted because I was baiting him. It felt like preparing to place a winning punch in a fight. I brushed the Vaseline off of his eyebrows with light enough comments to let him feel the pressure and cleared the spot to land the knockout blow. Nebraska would do that for me. I would watch Shrinker as the clock ran out. I would see him suffer. Every good dog has his day. The frustrating part was hard to imagine — Mr. Shrinker never recognized that I knew football.

Taped Up To Play

A bitter cold northerner arrived in Memphis for the Liberty Bowl football game. I sat in the wheelchair and tried to adjust my external catheter so that the glue would quit pulling pubic hair out, but it didn't work. When they loaded us on the bus, excitement filled my body in the darkness as we proceeded to the stadium. A rock hard freeze kicked off spasms and made the trip a challenge.

A shy woman leaned over my shoulder and surprised me. She asked, "Would you like this to keep warm?" She put a knitted orange and blue throw on top of me and the government blanket.

"Thank you very much," I responded.

She sat down behind me and my neck brace kept me from seeing her. I thought about her and wished we could talk. I wondered about her son who had died in Vietnam. How was he killed? I prayed for her. What was her name? What was his?

We approached the stadium and the pageantry of college football unfolded in euphoria. The first things we saw were retina-burning stadium lights and festive, happy throngs of tailgaters. Then, dense crowds in colorful clothing jammed the entries. I watched with happiness as the band drummed out a war beat. Our hospital bus parked and they began to unload us in reverse order.

They placed us along the wall at the far corner of the end zone. Not choice seats, but it tickled me to be there. I absorbed the atmosphere and watched the players warm up. Sporting blue and white, Carolina receivers caught perfect spirals. The stands filled to the brim and fans seemed to step into the sky. I could not see well to the Cornhuskers' end of the field, but I admired them from a distance. The big N on their helmets looked so simple. Monstrous sized humans wearing red and white, they seemed bigger than the North Carolina team.

The announcer's voice blasted across the crisp, bright-lit sky. "Good evening, ladies and gentlemen. Welcome to the 19th Annual Liberty Bowl." I perked up at the quality of the sound system created for the halftime tribute to Elvis.

I cheered from the heart and gut, but I sounded like a sick kitten. To my astonishment, my lungs were too weak from paralysis in my chest muscles to make noise. No more cheers were attempted.

I looked for Shrinker. All I saw from the VA Spinal Center were the guys in wheelchairs to either side of me. The staff sat far away to give us space but close enough to keep an eye on us. The Mothers of the Vietnam Veterans were elsewhere. We all appeared isolated and somber in our wheelchairs. I wanted to get up, dance and holler along the sideline to match my happy mood, but I was not able. Nobody else came around us—or even looked our way. Many looked away. I couldn't budge an inch on the grass in my wheelchair. Even so, I felt fine. Why sweat the small stuff?

The teams left the field for pre-game festivities and the crowd erupted in a deafening roar. I lapped it up. The band led out before the color guard. It moved me to see the American flag presented. The frosty air felt good to my nose. I hated not being able to stand up for the anthem. The Liberty Bowl staff gave out 50,000 American flags and the flickering mass of red, white and blue made a spectacular scene.

A crash of audio filled the evening air as the teams returned to the field to kick off the ball. The players lined up to wait for the return of the television audience. The athletes hopped up and down to pump adrenaline, anxious to hit somebody. Kick off renewed me more than anything since being paralyzed.

Carolina moved the ball at will and one might think they would soon have fifty points. Chuckling, I judged the Carolina fans and figured they had printed early headlines in their honor. Nebraska bent but didn't break over the years. North Carolina took the lead but the Cornhusker smash-mouth running game showed signs of life. Nebraska fullback Dodie Donnell scored a touchdown on a fifteen-yard scamper. Coach Osborne was not ready to forfeit yet. The Tar Heels scored with pass plays in the second quarter to stretch their lead and the scoreboard at halftime showed North Carolina ahead, 14-7.

The halftime show was incredible. God's spirit was present. They broadcast the life of Elvis Presley—and the story moved everyone. A true southern boy, Elvis made it from a shack in Tupelo to his Graceland mansion. He served his country in the Army. We felt unified when he sang. "Don't Be Cruel" flashed me back to the fifties when I watched my brother and sister of high school age dance in our living room to that song on a 78-RPM record. Roy Orbison performed live.

Anchored in a wheelchair, I sat smack dab in Dixie Land as part of the tribute to Elvis. Outside for the first time in three months, I was awestruck. While no one watched, I had gone through a metamorphosis since October 21, 1977. I could not forgive myself, but asked God to do so and to take the load off. Since being hurt, I covered over like a pearl to hide my value and protect my heart. Without voice, I begged God to set me free and make something of me—in his power and honor. I knew it would not happen overnight, but I had faith it would happen. I listened to Elvis Presley's God-gifted voice and a peace came over me. The Holy Spirit returned. I cried with happiness. This was a memorable night and like always, I was closest to God outdoors.

The second half of football became a slug fest. North Carolina extended the lead to 17 – 7 going into the final quarter. I think I saw some intestine blow out of the back end of a North Carolina receiver as the free safety rocked him on a crossing pattern. The stage was set for momentum to swing to the Cornhuskers. Their second team quarterback came in to throw and try to achieve victory. Nebraska crossed the end zone and caused 40,000 Carolina butts to pucker. The Tar Heels held on to the 17 – 14 lead. With three minutes to go, Nebraska began a relentless march down the field. So many times before, Nebraska castrated you and handed your pair back at the buzzer. The crowd went hysterical. I was frozen stiff but actively involved. Someone grabbed my wheelchair from behind and headed me out of the stadium.

"Back on the bus," they said.

"Are you shitting me?" I said as play continued behind me.

They rolled me past Mr. Shrinker. He said, "It's over. Back on the bus."

Shrinker chapped my ass again. I wanted to tie a half-hitch in his.

Nobody had a radio on the bus. I looked for the nice lady who had made my blanket but couldn't find her. I never saw her again. Many years have passed and the gift she gave is my keepsake.

I thawed-out back in my room and picked up the game recap on TV. Nebraska finished that last drive and won. Exhausted from the outing, I thanked God for a wonderful time and slept more soundly than a bear in hibernation.

Identity Crisis

Fish swim to fresh blue water. They enjoy a habitat that allows cover and the security to suspend and relax their metabolism. When they eat, they can be ferocious. Many times fish disguise themselves to blend into their surroundings. If pressured, they move on. A fish is aware of the bigger fish in the food chain. When necessary, a fish can swim with great strength and agility. Sometimes they are bottom dwellers and live on stink bait. From the stink bait come many of the strongest species.

I had no way to swim to blue water, living in a fish bowl at the VA Spinal Center but survived within this habitat. My cover was limited, but secure. Although my weight plunged, I never stopped eating. I survived many shark feedings and relocating from the bigger fish came naturally. Strength returned—agility would follow. An obvious bottom dweller, I was also a stronger species. My goal was to become the most robust of my species—and my faith determined that God delivers provision.

"Here, put this on," the nurse directed as she handed me a soft collar brace. "You can take it off to sleep," she said.

The soft cushion took pressure off my jaw and caused no pain like the other neck braces and Stryker frame strap. Even with slow hands, I could close the Velcro. I rolled down to PT wearing my new neck brace. My sister and brother planned to come for the New Year. I hoped to walk for them. I asked Phylisine if we could get me where I could walk alone in the bars.

"Let's try," Phylisine said.

Each evening I collapsed in bed without success, but I prayed that patience would pay off. Few people with spinal injuries ever have a chance to try to walk. I would reach the walking goal—even if it took months.

Christmas came and went. I remembered nothing about it. My sister's family arrived for New Year's. I went with them in a wheelchair and used a timer to remind me to adjust and avoid pressure sores. We went to a house in the country and my brother John's clan joined us. John and I posed as if arm wrestling and Bev snapped a picture. She took the picture back to Oklahoma City to show the staff at the VA Ward 7 North nursing station. They could not place me, but they sure remembered my brother. With our bellies full, they returned me to the center and drove home.

My hinged leg brace arrived. It kept my right foot from dropping and allowed my foot to rise as I stepped under my hip. I was delighted and saddened to get the metal hinged brace. I wanted a brace in my own shoe. They put it in a black military dress shoe, according to VA policy. I looked like a nerd with the shoes on. My severe spasticity caused my foot to oscillate in clonus —a quick reverberating motion. The metal brace squeaked as my foot hopped. The squeaking brace and other changes brought back memories of a healthy Hodge.

Frustrated, I reflected on the treatment of patients. The night I snapped my neck, I had on my favorite Wellington boots that weighed ten pounds and a pair of custom fit overalls. Now I wore black military dress shoes everywhere. I looked stupid in shorts going to PT and to aquatics in a swimsuit. I felt like a real stud in my brown paper bag-colored shirt, baggy swim trunks, white socks and noisy-ass black military dress shoes. I didn't need a psychiatrist to figure out that I was losing my identity. Why did the system lack focus on issues like dignity? Why was there a void at being personable? These valuable additions wouldn't take much effort. I thought it all over and started a list of these questions. Unlike Toto and Dorothy, I couldn't click my heels together and pray that it was only a dream.

Revised Agenda

I labored through the cold part of winter. By then, I was able to swim a few strokes and not drown in aquatic therapy. Neck pain killed me. It took all I had to get to my room after aquatics. I set a goal to swim one length of the small pool by the time of discharge at the end of February, but I did not accomplish that ambition. To try every day for months and not swim was disheartening, but I didn't stop. The buoyancy of the water allowed me to isolate weak muscle groups and exercise them until they were spent. Without aquatic therapy, I don't believe that I would have regained the flexibility and control to walk again.

One night, Shrinker took us out to the community wrestling show. The grappling pair spilled out into the crowd and around the corner—out of sight from where they parked us in our wheelchairs. I had learned in PT to walk outside the bars a little way using my cane and brace. As the outside-ring wrestling moved to the side of us, I stood up and took a few steps to look at the bogus entertainment. Mr. Shrinker directed the wrath of God at me. He yelled, "Get back in your wheelchair! Get back! Don't you know you could get hurt getting out of that wheelchair?"

That was all I could take. Hospital abuse came in many ways. It was physical, like the harsh treatment that I received in the VA in Oklahoma City, or mental, as the Shrinker gave to patients like me.

I seized control from the system and looked at Shrinker for what seemed like an hour without speaking, just studying his face. It was obvious we stepped all over each other's toes every time we tried to dance. He couldn't be my partner anymore. I thought about what his words meant. Did I know that I could get hurt getting out of this wheelchair? I was not in any danger—not even near the show. Getting out of a wheelchair wasn't risky. PT had cleared me to go the few feet I was traveling. Did Mr. Shrinker feel obligated to keep me in a chair so I wouldn't get hurt? I damned sure wasn't going to stay in one for him.

Shrinker saw my fury. "You just won't be invited out again."

We thought alike for once.

I could see "Shrinking Group" in the rear view from that instant on. Outings took place without me and I lived with it. I wondered how Mr. Shrinker got lucky enough to attend college. How did he get away with mistreating patients? Being an inpatient showed me that the authorities could act like Genghis Khan. Why not ask the sick and injured how their families were doing? Talk about hobbies or the good times. It sure beats brow-beating them for having their heads in their asses. I almost had mine pulled out and could see daylight. Wouldn't a few atta-boys go a long way?

Running On Empty

When they unlocked the door each day, I got in the parallel bars. Using what I gained in PT, I went back and forth until I dropped. As time passed, I covered longer distances outside the bars with my cane. Outings were lost so I created my own.

The huge VA parking lots emptied after the day workers left and on weekends. I enjoyed being outside and started making brief walks to sit on benches. Once stronger, I used light poles as distance measures. I counted them and added more when able to. The count went on day or night. I enjoyed the solitude and fresh air. Michael P sent me the new "Running on Empty" cassette[1]. With my headsets on in the empty lot, I was walking!

As my balance improved, I created a game of adapted golf. The light poles were holes. A large, round piece of gravel made a golf ball and my cane was a club. In this primitive sport, I entertained myself with chip shots. The game gave me a way to measure my progress and create new challenges until discharge. It helped me to learn hard lessons like dealing with soiled pants while being outside. As the weeks passed, this burden became more tolerable. Cleaning up with the wrong hand, leaning over and fighting not to fall off the commode, and keeping my numb fingers clean became easier, as did numerous other unspoken issues. Incomplete bowel and bladder control became a part of my life.

Crazy on You

Missing Barbara was hard to take. She was always on my mind. One day Michael P called and said, "We are gonna drive right out there this weekend and spend the day." He was bringing Barb and another old friend, Bob Cunningham.

Time could not go fast enough. They left Oklahoma as a huge ice storm and snow blizzard blanketed the path to Tennessee. I watched the weather on TV and through the hospital window.

---

1 Forrest Gump ran to the music later in movie life.

Much of their travel was going to be on closed roads at less than thirty-five miles per hour. I sat alone and the hours ticked by.

When they finally arrived, I apologized for asking them to come so far to see me. Michael had none of it. "Big deal—on I-40, you don't turn for a thousand miles until you hit Memphis." They went to the Willie Nelson concert before they left. "We listened to Willie sing 'Whiskey River' with the Texas Star alongside the American flag. Yeah man, a patriotic effect came on us as we got in the car to come here. The drive was a piece of cake."

Michael P looked exhausted and his description of their trip haunted me. I knew it had been no piece of cake. Their eyes looked like road maps from the all night drive in very dangerous conditions, but I was grateful to Michael P for risking it and glad to see them.

Barbara and I captured one another in a hug and kiss. She smelled good and felt soft. Her warmth took me like a puppy. Michael P and Bob went away for a few minutes. Barb and I closed the curtain in my open-air, multi-bed room. We were intimate and her sensuous kiss aroused me. There is a time and a place for everything and behind the curtain in a hospital bed was not the time and place.

We drove to a motel to be away from the Spinal Center. With great difficulty, both men helped me get across the ice and snow into the room. They lay down. Barbara followed us in and looked beat. It wouldn't be a long, relaxed visit like I had imagined.

The snow crossing took my legs, so my two buddies had to help me get to the bathroom. I finished taking a leak and signaled at Barbara to come into the small bathroom. There wasn't any private space in the motel room and the blizzard denied the guys a walk. I had visions of sex and romance after living caged for months. I knew my intentions were stupid, but Barbie submitted to touch and view for a short time. We knew our bathroom meeting was far too awkward—again the wrong time, wrong place.

I couldn't believe that this wrong place followed the last wrong place where we kissed behind my room curtain. Damn the luck. Two poor people searching for privacy and coming up empty handed. It seemed dumb, but I felt good that Barbie was kind enough to try — and I now had success maintaining an erection.

Michael P and Bob were sleepy as Barbie and I walked out of the motel bathroom. They stared dumbfounded and didn't know what to do as Barb helped me walk for the first time in our life. None of us ever expected to see her help me walk. We all thought this at the same time without even speaking a word.

They shared being bone-tired. My three months of confinement with injury and illness were a challenge to all of us. I was thankful that they had made it to see me, but aware of their shabby physical and mental status. The clock seemed to be ticking out loud. I knew my company had to return that same day to Oklahoma. The storm reduced the time we had together — and that broke my heart.

Back in my room, a cold, lonely feeling hit me. I had missed Barbara like good weather. It was great to see her, but I knew that the future was going to be rough and realized that she knew it, too. The song by Heart, "Crazy on You," went through my mind. Barbara and I had listened to the song. It turned us on and was one of our favorites — but now I sensed far different emotions from this music than the ones we shared before my wreck.

What to Do?

One February morning Dr. Workman, the physician in charge, met me in the hall. He was clowning around, laughing at me and mimicking my walking gait. I looked like Mr. Machine as my spastic legs moved with each step. My right foot was stuck in rapid clonus and the brace went squeaking along as my foot bounced out of control. I did look funny.

Dr. Workman said, "You're about ready to go home aren't you?"

I didn't know. I said, "Whenever you're ready."

I used my wheelchair less and less, but still needed it to last a full day. I rolled to the Occupational Therapy Department and began to lace a billfold, learning to use my left hand and teeth. I had learned to print with my left hand. My right hand was too weak and spastic—even with writing aids. As I worked, my therapist came over.

"The colonel wants to see you," she said.

I rolled my wheelchair under the sign at the office that read, "Chief of Occupational Therapy." The retired Army colonel seldom asked anyone into his office. I felt like I might have done something wrong.

The chief smiled. "What are you going to do when you get out of here?"

Now that was a good question. I pondered it for quite sometime, looked at my wheelchair and replied, "Walk."

The colonel reacted. "No, I mean for a living!"

I had not thought about that. Generally, I felt worthless. Throwing glass-bottled pop off a truck wasn't an option anymore. Looking ahead to work hadn't even crossed my mind. I swallowed hard and said, "I don't know, sir. What do you suggest?"

The old chief spoke volumes with just a few words. "You would make a good occupational therapist. You have good social skills."

He spoke of school requirements that scared me. A working man doesn't consider this stuff alone, but I was inspired that someone thought I could do something and thankful for the dignified approach. I said, "Thank you sir, I will check into it."

What he said was food for thought and well worth the ten minutes he gave me. Being an occupational therapist was a great option since no others came to mind. It could lead from down and out to up and in. I would do it.

At discharge, I asked to review my medication list and couldn't believe it when I read what they fed me. I addressed my concerns. "I can't stop going. Why do I need two bowel softeners?"

The nurse replied, "People in your condition live very sedentary lives and are prone to impaction."

My plumbing never clogged up. I replied, "I am busier than a beaver and plan to be busier. I don't need any stool softeners."

"That is for the doctor to decide," she said.

After months of inconsiderate directions in the hospital, I was tired. "Please tell Dr. Workman to take them himself — I won't be."

Disability Took Nothing Away

My hands could not move well enough to close buttons and I didn't want to use the slow button aid. I slipped on my pullover shirt and remembered my western shirts with the pearl inlay on the snaps that I had at home. They would be hard to close. I pulled up my sweat pants with the elastic waistband and rode a memory of the leather belt with my name engraved that I could no longer wear. Before I got hurt, I looked sharp wearing Wrangler jeans and Wellington boots. My foot slid inside the elastic strings that held my black military shoes on and spurred a thought about how tough it would be to bend over and lace shoestrings. After tightening the strap on my ankle brace, I balanced on my cane and walked to say good-bye at the front desk. That last night at home, my weight was a solid one hundred eighty-five pounds. After six months in the hospital, I limped back to my world in Oklahoma at a frail one hundred thirty-five. Only a portion of my confidence returned in another body. Last October, no one could beat me. Now I was humbled and accepting of my fate. God had a plan and I'd carry it out.

Oklahoma was a foreign land that no longer felt right to me. A stone body drained my energy. It seemed like a lot more time passed than did — just short of an eternity. Loneliness stayed with me after my arrival. These strange impressions hit hard and early because I had yet to get to my house.

At the curb, my basset hound caught my scent. Walter barked in nervous anticipation. I felt the same way. I wanted to hurry to the backyard but had one slow gear. I listened to him howl with glee over my homecoming. There was no handrail and I couldn't get up the two steps. Barbie helped me with a hug—but it was different than before and mysterious. I used to lift her up off her feet. Now she had to help keep me on mine.

Walter continued to bellow and Barb let him in the back door. He met me with compassion like always, but this time he knocked me down with a slobbery licking in the face. I couldn't overpower him as before. Nevertheless, love still ran through our touch. With our carefree physical contact, disability took nothing away.

Barbara and I talked about the small things that had happened while I was away. We laughed and she caught me up on the latest. Soon enough, we made for our bed. Adaptation was necessary. I could only caress her with my left hand, so she snuggled to the right even though that was backwards from our normal routine. We fooled around with carnal feelings. I tried—but couldn't balance on top or sideways. Hugs and kisses were still lusty rewards. It was awkward taking off each other's clothes, but the heat was rising. Being naked remained a thrilling, sensuous treat. Human touch plays like an orchestra. Barbara and I discovered we were out of tune and our old spontaneous ways were gone.

We made love with me on bottom. We made love and made love. Barbie climaxed. After awhile, I asked that she help me achieve orgasm, but couldn't do so. I never would with her again, just like Mr. Shrinker said. Suddenly, my bowels moved before I could get up. Barb helped clean. She cared so much. It destroyed me and I never overcame it. Disability took away so many things.

Four – Nursing

Jet on a Jaguar

I filled my lungs with the sweet fragrance of the morning air that poured through the window. Paying a fee for it would have been acceptable. My pain levels were severe and the spasms awakened Barb. She stretched naked on her feet at the side of the bed.

"How are you?" she asked.

"Fine. Did you sleep well?"

She nodded yes and readied for work.

I adjusted to home sweet home. My '69 GMC pickup had a left foot accelerator now because my right leg was too paralyzed. I liked driving again, but strength and balance were poor when I tried turning corners. Caution ruled my world. The truck cab seemed large.

Mike Kuns set up outpatient therapy at the VA Hospital and I steered towards the torture chamber, wondering why I chanced it. Pulling in to the huge VA parking lot felt like re-entering my worst nightmare. I began the chore of going around and around the congested area to find a parking spot. Just being near the place gave me the creeps and it took courage not to dart away. If someone yelled boo, they would have to use a putty knife to chip my remnants out of the cab headliner. I was tenser than a cat in a dog pound.

I sat in the lobby. A veteran in a wheelchair smoked a cigarette through his throat tube. Men lay on the floor. Everyone was discouraged with waiting. The war was over and many of the vets were young. The place overflowed with cigarette smoke and filthy men. I went back to Ward 7 North but nobody knew me. They never saw me on my feet and it threw them. After one therapy appointment, I never went back.

Each morning at six, I stretched in the YMCA pool, swam better and adapted a light lifting program. This disciplined start was good. It took practice to pick up weights, pull and place pins, relocate positions—and socialize. These demands helped me evolve. Within four weeks I reached a goal. I could swim one full length of the pool without stopping. I added pool lengths over time and learned to live again.

I took giant steps. I drove through the Medical Center to find the College of Health. The first test was finding a place to park—handicapped or not. Close by the college, I almost peed on myself trying to pull over to jettison fuel into my urinal. Once out of traffic, I relieved my spastic bladder, tossed the contents below the truck door and expanded my thinking about how I didn't fit in at the Medical Center. I tied my pony up and strolled in to find out what the requirements were for acceptance into the Oklahoma University Health Sciences Center School of Occupational Therapy.

To get an entry interview for the OT program was a long shot. Many students applied, few made it. I liked the challenge—but "Mr. Reality" teaches hard lessons and I had a Masters Degree from his school. For the OT program, a three point five grade point average was required in science courses. I needed to complete those classes in summer session and make straight A's to jack up my grade point. After tucking all of that under my belt, the OT Search Committee had to pick me to start school in the fall of 1979. It sounded easy—like landing a jumbo jet on a jaguar.

I could enter the College of Health after I finished the summer session. The OT course staples were hard to digest. We would take classes ranging from orthopedics to anatomy, with human dissection lab. I could skin a buck but never considered a human. The whole notion overwhelmed me. I asked myself a thousand times if I was fooling myself. I looked forward and backward. The OT profession was comprised mainly of females. I had never been in that kind of crowd before. Lab required standing three hours a day. I was challenged to stand at the men's urinal long enough to piss. The drop-out rate was high. The books and coursework were expensive. I heard that you had to prove financial means to finish. A maimed man who was short on money had a lot to consider. I still wanted to drink beer and ride motorcycles. Before I got hurt, canned chili and beanie weenies kept me strong and happy. I had the confidence of a lion. Nothing was certain now and I watched each bite to ensure that I had enough strength to make the day. Sadly, getting to the restroom was a favorite past time. I acted like the Scarecrow in the **Wizard of Oz** and walked like the Tin Man. My disability income was meager. I stopped to add up all I didn't have and saw that the OT notion couldn't work.

Blown away and unable to believe getting through OT school was possible, I needed encouragement and prayed for energy, expertise, health and money to complete the coursework. One thing was sure, God had to take the lead for a lame brain like me to get through. Blind faith kept me going. Nothing was familiar at a jugular level. Two things became evident as I headed toward the junior college that I had attended earlier. First, my old self had vanished, except in memory. Second, I had a vision of the new one.

Charles Farr was a vocational counselor at the junior college. He said my GI benefits would help and my disabled condition qualified me for financial aid. Mr. Farr voiced concern. "I've never had anyone succeed in those high level medical courses."

I could see why, but stayed optimistic—and followed the Spirit. I said, "I think I can do it if given the chance."

He reviewed my file and emphasized the large expenses for my selected field. Mr. Farr gave me a dead-sober offer. "Succeed one semester at a time or funding will cease." Two years later, he nominated me for the recognition award, "Most Outstanding Disabled Person in Oklahoma."

God opened a door that I would never have entered had it not been for my "brokenness." He broke me to build me to bless me. Now I could be a blessing to others. We are like horses to some degree. Saddling me and getting a bit in my mouth came hard but I galloped ahead on a path of destiny.

Dumb as a Rock

I told Barbara that my VA man would pay for school. She was delighted with the news. I mapped out a wild-eyed proposal that turned out to be an adventure of mind and body.

I said, "Let's take a trip to Bull Shoals in Arkansas!" I detailed my fantasies. "I've never been there. We'll hook up your folk's boat and stay a few days before I start school. Dr. Schoenhals told me last week I could do whatever I wanted because my neck fusion is healed and stronger than the original. I work out every day. Let's take the inner tube — I want to see if I can ride it!"

Barb shared none of my enthusiasm. She was scared of my ideas and she hesitated a long time. "Hodge, I don't think you're ready. I'm not ready."

"Oh, come on Barbie — we need a vacation!"

"What about the money?"

"We can scrape it together."

She was right. I wasn't ready. I did my best to prepare to leave, but wore out getting things together. Barbara got the groceries, hooked up the boat, loaded the truck and tended to details that I had taken care of before. We left tired. Unable to accept all my new limits, I pushed on. I turned down her offer to drive. Sitting up was hard after a short while. Stubborn mules are hard to manage.

The first part of the trip was a straight shot and at least we had time to visit. We talked as we had in the past, never going into detail about anything of present relevance. Taking a trip this quick in recovery was a sure sign that I possessed no intelligence. Rather

Chum Water

than take a road trip, I should have spent time at home, resting and recuperating. Yes, sitting in the shade with Barbara would have been a wise choice, but nobody ever accused me of being smart. In fact, I was as dumb as a rock. I lost all signs of grace down the road as my body quit working.

"Holy shit," I exclaimed as I read the caution sign entering the mountains in Arkansas.

The sign had curly-cues describing the sharp turning road ahead. It read, "Steep and Hazardous Next 23 Miles." I gulped as I passed the warning sign. I had already been leaning into the door on easy right curves—and hanging onto the steering column to correct my balance curving left. Now the roads were steep and narrow with sharp turns. With no shoulder on the road to pull the truck and boat trailer onto, we weren't going to come out alive. I was scared and it obviously alarmed Barb. My emotions headed as far out of control as my physical abilities had changed.

With mile one gone and twenty-two more to go, I glanced at Barb and made an honest request. "Would you pray for us, please?"

I drove through the twisting route imagining the worse. What if the truck had a mechanical problem? What if the trailer came loose from the ball or the boat yanked loose from the trailer? I thought the receiver hitch was loose, imagined we were going to eat the front end of an oncoming logging truck and told Barbara that she should have never allowed me to go on the trip in the first place. This fish was flopping around on the bank. My bladder kicked off in spasm as I steered through the mountainous curves. Barb got on-the-job training in dick retrieval and urinal alignment during an active road race. Neither of us hesitated to speak our minds while we rode and held on for dear life. As I watched the odometer tick off the last mile, I thanked the Lord for the clear shot I saw ahead. My left foot was tired from hitting the pedals. I quit hallucinating over things falling apart when I realized that God had saved us. We had survived miles of self-applied road rage.

There was a stretch of straight road. Silence mastered the day. I closed in on another sign. More curves ahead. I barked out an order more deliberate than General Patton. "Barbara, you're driving!"

There was a scenic pullover for honeymooners like us. I found the break with my left foot and parked. I looked at Barbara. She looked at me. I made a confession and request. "I am sorry for bringing you here. Could you get us there?"

"I don't know if I can pull the boat through these curves," she muttered.

"Let's catch some air, okay?"

"Yeah." Barbara stepped towards the green forest.

I struggled to get out of the truck and fell flat on my ass. My legs didn't hold. I looked up and down the road, fearful that someone thought I was drunk. There were no cars. I tried to stand several times but couldn't get up. I looked under the truck at Barb's backside and asked for help. She got me in and helped scoot me over. We looked at one another, clinched in a hug and cried bitter tears. Life wounded us and there was nothing more to say.

Carefree Energy

We slept like the dead and awoke to find the beauty of the Arkansas outdoors. Like a cloud, the fog rolled thick and high above the crystal clear lake. We marveled at the transparency, the cold air and the purity. Barb was energetic but my body felt like it had been in a fistfight. My injured spinal cord burned my hands and feet. I said nothing about it, took my licks—and kept going.

Brother John met us, and together they helped me get in the boat. We took off across the water and the force threw me around. The motion of the powerboat on throttle was wonderful. I laughed out loud, but noticed a change. Barb and John weren't as carefree. They worried about me.

Chum Water

We anchored. Barb smiled and said it was too cold for her to ski. I explored my sea legs. The water moving under the boat had the effect of standing on a trampoline. The slightest ripple against the hull tossed me like a kid on a teeter-totter. I had to hold on to balance. Nobody was on the lake—and I felt very distant from my companions. I scanned across the surface. It was strange.

The spirit came upon me to be thrilled. "I think I will ride that inner tube again."

Barbara and John looked at each other with nothing to say. It gave me the impression that they thought they had five minutes to live. I couldn't blame them and let some time pass.

Barb and John acquiesced and I gave them instructions on how to help me. I needed complete assistance in and out of the boat. They confirmed their willingness—but I could see the doubt in their eyes. Mounting the tube was a challenge, but I knew I could ride it. I had dreamed about it a hundred times in recovery. Now it was time. My adrenaline pumped. Falling off didn't scare or concern me—my neck was fused well. We began the process together. They helped me get my life jacket strapped and supported me while I stretched. Excited and cold, my right foot began to bounce with clonus and that concerned them.

The clonus passed and I said, "Steady me on the side and I'll fall in." I added reluctantly, "Oh, one other thing—kind of keep an eye out for my right hand getting hung up in the tow rope—I wouldn't be able to get it out."

They complied like they were putting me in shark infested water with chum strapped to my chest. I recognized their fear and zoned it out. I focused on entering the water, where gravity was not a problem.

Back in the Saddle Again

The splash in the frigid water took my breath and increased my spasticity. I was wound tighter than a golf ball.

After many tries, I mounted the inner tube and found a position to ride. That was the hard part. Then, focusing on the boat, I paid attention to remaining balanced while idling out into the lake. When everything was perfect, I yelled, "Hit it!"

The tube reared back and plopped down to plane on the water. I rode behind a boat again with sheer pleasure. Watching the water skim by below me was a blast. The water on my face drove backwards and the forces plastered my hair in a slick. The clatter of the tube against ripples sounded great. My left hand had a monkey grip and this strong arm provided adjustments as the tube bounced. My right hand drew up into the handle and I had no way to let go. My strength was gone as soon as I started. I tried to reposition myself so as to undo my right hand. A wave surprised me and jabbed me in the gut. I tipped into the water for an immediate end to the tube tow. The return to paradise was brief.

The cold water refreshed me—and I tossed around in joy. My right foot spasmed away. I exhaled under water and watched the bubbles escape from my nose. Life was once again fabulous and there were no cares. I heard the scream of the boat prop churning water and heading back. I righted myself—exhausted, but never happier. Paralyzed eight months ago, I had a short tube ride and a wonderful time. The fish was back in the lake.

The boat pulled up alongside me. John and Barb shouted, "Are you okay?" They looked scared stiff.

"You bet!" I said. "I rode the tube again!" I cheered and they laughed, clapped and cheered. I reached for the boat and said, "Hey, it's cold. Can you help me in?"

My right leg wouldn't go on the ladder. My teeth began to chatter. I reached up to John with my right hand and my arm curled back toward me in a tight, spastic position that was common with cord damage. John thought I had pulled back. I described my predicament and asked him to reach to me. I would never have been able to get back in the boat without their help.

They draped a towel around me. All was well, except I felt like a frozen shrimp. We all three relaxed. I was incapable of a second tube ride even if it paid a million dollars—but I did it once. I had glimpsed what the future might offer. I took a week to recover.

Crash Course

Arkansas was fun but I felt miserable to be so tired and in such pain. Although I was in great condition considering all things, I had severe strength loss due to the remaining paralysis. I felt no pain with scrapes on my left side. My legs were too weak to crouch and I couldn't lift my right heel up from the ground. Nobody understood and I quit trying to tell.

Barb and I drove back onto Oklahoma flat land. Cruise control saved the little bit of strength left in my good leg. Fatigue caused the foot to clonus and it was hard to hold down the pedal. My right arm couldn't steady the steering wheel. Something as simple as driving was hard. I glanced down at my soft stomach and noted that the tight grid that used to be there was gone. Thoughts came to mind of the past compared to now. My lungs once sucked in air like a vacuum and exhaled like a leaf blower during a boxing match. Now my right chest wall moved little because of paralysis. This day was mysterious in many ways. Driving with physical difficulty while reflecting on the changes was just the beginning.

I scanned the radio and found a country preacher. It was odd for me to listen to gospel radio. We went to church once in awhile and wanted a taste of the good water and forgiveness. However, neither of us grew in our Christian walk. An ominous air surrounded the cab and I could sense the various and opposite energies pulling us. All at once the cruise control malfunctioned and the truck charged ahead at full throttle. I thought for a minute that we were in for my latest disaster.

"Wow, the cruise stuck!" I explained.

I tapped the brake and the cruise released. I set it again with the same results.

Hodge Wood

"Looks like the cruise is out," I told her.

She looked at me like I was a stranger—and I changed the radio channel.

We made it home.

Barb returned to work the next morning.

I pulled on my Wellington boots with effort but couldn't take one step in them. It took time to put on my favorite western shirt with pearl snap buttons. It hung on me. I looked in the mirror at a POW. Off came my fancy clothes. I sat despondent, hating my looks. The reality lessons never stopped. Nobody understood.

A good buddy called and offered to come over and start jogging with me.

I said, "I can't bring my right leg through, so I can't jog."

"Hodge, you're being such a wimp."

He hung up and never came by.

I would have to love everyone anyway. They had no idea. I wanted to become good at loving again, but I wasn't there yet. The permanence and lack of understanding of my incomplete spinal cord injury cut to the bone.

I called Ruth Sanders to see if she could take up my western shirts. She had been like a mother. Growing up, I lived with her and her husband as much as with my mom and dad. They were survivors of the Great Depression. Ruth was plain and wore her thin red hair in a tight curl. She had natural beauty, a tender spirit—and spoke with a sweet Okie twang. She was a servant's servant.

Ruth came right over. She said, "Honey, I can take the chest and arms in on these shirts and you will look fine. I will be fixin' to sew 'em this week."

It felt good to think my pearl snap western shirts would fit, but I hated to be a bother. "Are you sure? I could buy smaller shirts."

The truth was I was tired of wearing pullover shirts and sweatpants. I could get jeans on. I asked, "Could you punch some holes in my cowboy belt so I can tighten it up?"

Ruth was pleased to help.

I told her I was going to get a new leg brace that would fit in my own shoes called an ankle foot orthosis. I could toss the metal brace and goofy black shoes in the trash. I shared how good I would feel dressed like me.

Ruth had no great understanding of braces but replied without hesitation. "That'll be real nice, Sugar. Can I take some laundry back and do it?"

She was happy to drive away with my shirts and laundry to wash by hand in her garage.

Save My Life

Hot summer progressed. One evening, Barb and I met some friends at a beer bar. Ruth hadn't finished my clothes, so I still dressed like a clown in a weirdo carnival. I had fears that I hadn't voiced. I was unable to cope with loud noises or crowds since I got out of rehab. Any loud place—a house full of people or a busy retail store—scared me. Raw energy in a crowd plugged me in to a wall socket. Bars were noisy places that sat off alarms.

Barbie and I paid the bouncer and stepped into the bar. The air conditioning and darkness created a drastic contrast to the bright hot day. I lost my balance on a carpet wrinkle, leaned into my cane and tried to adjust my eyes. Two long-haired bikers in leather were leaving and their cigarette smoke cut my breath. I heard Harleys crank over behind the door and the sound made me shiver. It seemed as if the temperature dropped ninety degrees. The band's drummer was a friend named Greg and they were getting ready to begin a set.

I stumbled to the bathroom before pausing to sit down at our table. The band launched into a song, "Save my life I'm going down for the last time." The music and setting were over stimulating. Rigidly, I stood in place, unable to move.

Friends observed me as the band rocked. I glanced at myself. I had on my black military shoes with the pewter metal brace, white socks, a pair of lime green cotton shorts and a green and yellow striped pullover that I had bought from Wal-Mart. Everyone in the beer joint noticed how far out of place I looked. I couldn't sit down, frozen in fear and spooked by the energy. Barbara looked flat and distant. I couldn't move. With work, I sat down.

Someone raised a pitcher and filled my glass. I reached right handed to get the draw as I would before I got hurt—forgetting I had to use my left hand now. My right hand would not open around the glass, so I withdrew it and my motions were strange.

Greg finished the final lead vocal line to the song with power. He stuffed his drumstick onto the top of the skin with the last beat and announced, "That was dedicated to my friend right there, Hodge Wood—'Save my life I'm going down for the last time.'" Greg stood as if to welcome royalty and aimed his drum stick at me. You could have heard a pin drop.

Anxiety froze me and I barely mustered a nod of thanks to Greg. A few people clapped at his recognition, but most of the crowd wondered why the drummer dedicated the song to the weirdo in the green shirt and black shoes. Not being able to cope with noise and crowds felt terrible. The alarms were more real than a punch in the nose. Even with several beers, I remained spooked. The spell didn't pass until we were leaving. I had no idea what to do about these fears that jumped into my head for no good reason. I wouldn't understand for another twenty-five years.

More Faster

Summer session at the junior college was a quick ride from my workouts. However, on most mornings, I just reached the bathroom before physiology class. "Mrs. Boredom" went at lightning speed—faster than my left hand could go. I flew through notes using printed scribbles. My writing went from bad to worse when I tried to go faster. I was fortunate to go to school, but it took extra hustle. I had never been shy about work and that quality paid off.

In physics, I sat next to Steve Faulk. We had attended high school together. He, like me at twenty-five, had taken some detours before getting serious about college. Steve had a sense of humor and could fist fight. We laughed about previous scraps.

"Steve, remember off-season football when you and Bevel hooked up? You yanked his shirt over his head, punched him blind and the blood flew." The fight went on for thirty minutes and the janitor sat down to watch. Bevel loved to fight.

Steve cackled, "Yeah, we fought because I told Bevel you whipped his ass twice—when Looney stepped between you and had stitches put in his ear and when you two boxed."

"Yeah, he's a fighter. He knocked Michael P's front teeth out, you know?"

Steve became a dentist and his leadership in class gave me hope. As a high school kid, he came across without attention to the cultural aspects of life that professionals need. Now as a maturing adult he gained skills in those areas but never gave up the fun side that makes life far more entertaining.

I never got behind in school. Although I didn't agree with everything, the experience was excellent. At times the bullshit was deep. One teacher said that football players showed homosexual signs because they slapped each other on the ass. I gained tolerance. I grew, studied day and night and found a passion for learning. Soon they would interview me for entry into the Occupational Therapy Program at the Health Sciences Center. With both work and play, I had become productive again.

Barbara's brother-in-law, Johnny, was a plumber. He could be mean as a pit bull, but we got along okay and often went to the lake. We created a game called "More Faster" on the inner tube. I had advanced my riding skills and challenged him to compete. I wanted to eliminate complaints.

I said, "Johnny, let me whip you across the lake as fast and as hard as I can. You can't say a word, except 'more faster.' When you have all you need, switch and pull me. I say the same or quit."

Johnny loved the chance to try to kill me. We could wrench each other up in whips. The rest of the family laughed at our ignorance. Considering the limits of a paralyzing spinal injury, I had worked back into tip-top shape by summer's end. Although this fish still couldn't swim strong, he was "King of the Tube." A chosen few ride a tube behind a boat. There is a required zone you must get into while holding on to an inflated doughnut tied to a tow bar. I could get into the zone. If a tuber can't find the zone, prayer dominates thought — and getting off is the answer to prayer.

I positioned up on the inner tube in the hot sun. "Idle out, Johnny."

I clinched the tube handles and transferred the load to my left arm. With my mind set to hang on forever, Johnny couldn't sling me off. I scanned for boats, checked the wind and waves and yelled, "Hit it!"

Prepared for full throttle, I loaded up on adrenaline. The tube scooted away in the blink of an eye and I hung back to offset the pounding of the water. As Johnny turned hard, the inner tube stalled before darting across the wake. The wake burst the tube into the air and I flew above it. The rope whined with torque. Whipped and double throttled, the tube ricocheted out past the side of the boat as far as it would go. I knew the drill.

Johnny turned hard towards me and the boat crossed with maximum power. I glanced at his berserk smile as he flew by. The tube made an abrupt move at light speed. Colliding with the oncoming wake required me to predict how to land on the other side in an airborne instant. I calculated a position, shifted to land and used a split second to reset for the next swing the other way.

The rope tried to catch the boat but it had gone elsewhere, resulting in a hard whip that placed my tube in front of the boat on the other side. While the water grabbed at the tube, I dug in my left big toe like a rudder to maintain some form of control.

Johnny steered back again. I grazed the surface at warp speed as he created a full circle whip. I saw other boats' wakes. A full scan in one microsecond fed my brain and I counted twelve wakes that I would blast over. In that click of time, I created a plan for all the required position changes at what would feel like rocket speed.

I prepared to hit the twelve wakes. The rope shot me sideways and the tube gasped out an echo each time the water slapped it. Much of the time, I was airborne. I almost let my jaw fly open and I could have bitten my tongue off. It distracted me. I prepared to eject but regained my location in space, ramped across the next boat wake and continued.

Following the concave path of the towboat, I saw a large swirl in my personal space and the water blew me off without mercy. Relaxed and flying like a cannonball, I landed on my back as my legs continued in the direction that they were going when the tube was in my hands. The lake re-entry stopped my forward motion.

My swim trunks and jock had rolled up together on my thighs. I exhaled an exhausted laugh underwater, unraveled my swim wear and stretched out on my back. I floated and listened to my heart thumping with my ears below water. I was a nasty dog—a funky king—as ZZ Top sang on the Fandango vinyl.

The boat propped down beside me. Johnny smiled with fire in his eyes. He thought he had me. "What do you think?"

"More faster," I replied.

Funky King

Buoyancy was an equalizer and I was at home in water, but on land, my cord injury was evident. I couldn't carry my own weight once out of the water. After playing 'More Faster' and being tenderized, I felt like Gumby. Mud was a major obstacle. My cane stuck and I needed help to get to shore. Climbing was not possible —a slight embankment was too much. Falling was common. Barb and I had a tent on the lake shore. I needed her to get to camp. Barb did her best to act as if these issues were no big deal, but they were a big deal. I could sense her embarrassment and couldn't cope with mine.

I used to set up the tent, load the grill, carry the ice chests and perform the physical camp work. After tubing and boating in the sun, I sat to watch. It was all I could do to walk a few feet on level ground. Barbara had less time for me because she put more into the work involved in camping.

"La Grange" from ZZ Top's **Tres Hombres** album hammered through the evening sun into our public campsite. Barb knelt down in her bikini top to wipe down the underside of the boat. Her boobs bounced as she scrubbed. She was gorgeous in her skimpy cut-offs and her tight bottom pointed out. I leaned back in my lawn chair and enjoyed the scenery. Two men at the next campsite were enjoying the view, too. Not possessive or jealous before my wreck, I hated that they were watching Barbara. Worse, they had seen me and could care less. I didn't need another bad emotion to tend to, but I was incensed with jealousy. These guys horned in on me and Barb didn't seem to mind the attention.

After dark, I forgot about them. Everyone sat around the campfire. Barb held hands with me. The timbers glowed for hours, then turned to embers. We went to bed inside the tent and got naked. Lying down, I massaged Barbie's body. Her tan lines were distinct—even in the moonlight. We made love until we tired.

I listened to the crickets for awhile and asked, "Did you like those guys looking at you?"

"What do you mean—looking at you?"

"I mean in your bikini. Did you like them looking at you?"

"Oh Hodge, go to sleep. You worry too much."

I maintained touch for security. Barbie went to sleep. I worried for a while and dozed off.

Bacon and eggs smelled good the next morning. We were going back home after having a good time. The weather cooperated all weekend long but it was to change soon. While breaking camp, I looked Barb in the eyes and said, "Barb, I'm going to water ski again. Just give me some time to get well. I just need a little time."

Barbara looked back speechless and saddened. "Hodge, you can't ski."

"Yes, I know, but I will again someday."

She touched my cheek with her palm, became motionless and walked away without saying anything. I watched as she folded the card table and placed it in the truck. She reloaded our gear and never looked back. We didn't speak about me skiing again.

Fall arrived. My coursework increased and Barb gained greater responsibility at work. The fall turned to winter and Mother Nature took her wrath out. Barbara gained weight. I got depressed. We did have a nice Christmas at her parent's house. I got Barb a waist length white and black rabbit fur coat. She looked beautiful in it and the markings accented her hair. I was afraid to go anywhere New Year's Eve, but Barb went out and partied without me. Her indifference towards me grew more apparent and I showed anger towards her as my depression externalized. We had gone through more than most couples. We loved each other and weren't quitters, but I knew that separation was not far away.

A snowstorm blanketed us in January. I called Jimmy and asked if he had seen Barb, but he hadn't. Unable to walk in the snow, I was stuck in the house. We had traded for a newer Buick. Alone at home, with the snowfall burying us and with Barbara elsewhere, I perceived the Buick to be a priceless Mercedes and was certain she would wreck it in the storm. I worried she would get hurt and wasn't ready for that under any circumstances.

Barbara came in, lovely in her white fur and I unloaded. "Where have you been?" My tone was condemnatory.

"Nowhere, really"

"Barbie, I worry about you. You're always going somewhere."

She countered in defense. "We had a few drinks after work—that's all."

I lashed out. "Hell, you could kill yourself in this weather!"

"Not a bad idea. Give me some air, please." She walked into the bedroom.

The phone rang and it was Ruth about Tom. Tom had lung and lip cancer, with a lung removed a year ago. He had been doing okay. Ruth was pleasant. "I hate to bother you two sweeties, but Tom has been put in St. Anthony's Hospital and I can't drive. Could you please take me?"

Chum Water

I told Ruth we would be right over.

"Barb, I am awful sorry about getting mad at you. Tom is in Saints — and Ruth needs us to take her. I can't walk in this weather. Will you help me go help Ruth?" I said these words and tears came down my face. "Barbie, I am so sorry for everything."

Barbara looked at me blankly. "Let's go," she said.

Tom died that night with Ruth at his side. He was the best I knew — Tom took me fishing and hunting, made my baseball games — things Dad never did. That morning I sat next to his body and reflected back about our times past.

Tom's services were to take place in Atwood in the old schoolhouse in southeastern Oklahoma. The drive would take an hour and a half in good weather, but the snowstorm reached blizzard capacity. The Highway Patrol told me on the phone that the roads were impassable. They suggested no travel.

God made me mad and I had to ask, "Why bury such a fine man in a blizzard?" Tom and Ruth had no children. Most of the people who wanted to attend the service were elderly. The country roads were not going to be graded. The thought that no one could get through saddened me. Barb and I headed out in the storm. When we arrived, the little Atwood country school with inadequate heat and parking was overfilled. The car procession stretched for a mile to go place Tom in his grave. He had gone the extra mile for so many. Their need to mourn this man was deeper than the snow.

It was a cold time of year and a cold time in life. Funerals often have us examine where we are in life and trigger change. Change transpired on that blanket of snow. Barbara moved out to live with Jackie, a divorced girlfriend. While we were estranged, she totaled the Buick one night, but luckily wasn't injured. The wreck took more away from our damaged relationship than an insured hunk of metal. I wished she'd come back, but no relationship insurance can be purchased to restore the past. We made infrequent but civil contact, called on occasion and spent one awkward night together.

Hodge Wood

There was nothing more a ZZ Top "Funky King" could do, so I hung around and waited for some luck and a change in her heart.

Boiling Chemicals

Barb and I exchanged small talk at her apartment one spring day and a tall, masculine fellow named Steve arrived. He wore a wind suit with "Master Craft Boats" embroidered on the back, and Barb introduced him as Jackie's boyfriend. He stayed briefly, but long enough for me to learn that he had a boat and private lake house on his own small body of water. He sold Master Craft Competition Tournament Ski Boats. Steve looked to be everything I wanted to be. I wished him well as he left. Since Jackie was gone, Barb walked him out.

"Nice guy," I reflected to Barb as she re-entered alone.

"What does he see in Jackie? Her ass is fat."

Barb did not answer.

"By the way Barbie, you are looking terrific—you weigh less than when I met you and you're in great shape."

"They take me skiing."

The thunder rolled in storm after storm that spring. I stayed alone at home when not working out or at school. Although I had not seen or heard from Barbara in awhile, I still had hopes she would come back.

One day she did. I was excited to see her. Barb smiled as she ran inside, acting like she had never left. She placed a question before me that pulled the cord on my incestuous desires. "I bought a new leopard swimsuit—can I try it on?"

"Sure!"

She zipped by me to the bedroom. I had not been with a woman since she left. I turned and stood to the side, behind Barbara at the mirror in the daylight, expecting she had come to spend time with me. I was impressed with her erotic entry and became aroused as she got naked. My chemicals were boiling. I viewed her tanned body from the front in the mirror and from behind. She had her black hair styled short and sharp. She slipped the new, daring one-piece suit on with the labels still on it. She posed in various positions and looked at herself, then turned to me.

"How do I look?"

I experienced nuclear melt-down. I leapt forward to hold her expecting that the good times had returned.

"Oh, no, Hodge." Barb pulled away and acted surprised at my advance. "I bought the suit and was nearby and wanted to try it on." She pointed this out with an innocent air and with no sense of obligation. She assumed that was fine.

She turned to once again pose in the mirror before getting nude again. She placed the suit in the sales sack and dressed. I had never experienced anything like it. She wasn't being cruel. I was just a friend who lived nearby. Barbie said good-bye and that's the last time she came by the house. I am sure she recognized later that she hurt me. She didn't mean to. Neither of us had ever chosen to hurt one another. Life lays the lumber on us all the time and we go on.

Barb confessed that Steve was her fellow and that they water skied daily. I was disappointed and felt very small. I continued to work out hard, study and play my guitar as best I could with paralyzed hands. Otherwise it was a hermit's existence.

It was time for a curtain call. I couldn't tolerate not seeing Barb or waiting for her to come back, so I called and asked to deliver some silverware that she had left. Elaborate goodbyes were in my mind as I drove to our encounter, but at the meeting I realized that there was little to say. After placing the silverware in her trunk, we left to go find what else life had to offer, besides each other.

I headed towards my house and reflected on taking Barbara to the Fleetwood Mac concert when the *Rumor's* album was number one on the charts. We had neither paralysis nor death to consider then. Life was easy. I took Barb backstage for free, because I had been hired to work stage security. I was strong and a dependable front line bouncer. That night I helped singer Stevie Nicks walk up the stage steps before she performed. Barb and I were once happy. Now, as Fleetwood Mac would sing, we could go our own way.

Back home alone, I placed the record needle down on a Skynyrd tune, "Tuesday's Gone." It fit my mood. More aware than ever of my spinal injured body, I struggled to stand and balance at the turntable, bounced the needle on the album, stumbled to turn and sat back down in the dark. Considering myself a hopeless failure, I uncorked a fifth of Jack Daniels Black and placed it on the table. I loaded my .357 Magnum pistol and placed it in front of me next to the whiskey. In the dark, the blues overwhelmed me. Numbed by whiskey and music, I passed out somewhere along the way.

Days later, my lawyer sent divorce papers to the last woman who ever knew me on fast legs. Barbie signed them. We clocked out.

Licking Wounds Clean

Walter and I sat on the back porch and zoned out to music each evening that summer. My next-door neighbor Shorty talked to me over the fence and tried to raise my spirits. He was a lovable guy — a retired fireman with a bad back and good sense of humor.

Shorty had seen it all living next door. He was there when Michael P resided in the back bedroom and we partied all night. I remembered how the old fireman joked about the girls he watched come and go, including many from the future nursing class of '76 that Michael and I dated. This close neighbor saw me come in soaked in sweat from my delivery route at Pepsi and load my motorcycle and a six-pack to go race until late at night. Shorty watched me work with a crushed thumb and stitched head. I never missed a day of work because of weather or stitches or strains. My friend next door had seen me beat, cut and bruised but never beaten. After hitting hard times, my pardner next door offered me a few bucks when my Corvette turned into an old pickup. He saw me leave one day as a strong, street fighting man and return the next year skinny, in a brace and on a cane. Skynyrd sings that every mother's son will rise and fall someday. I proved it true.

One night that summer, Shorty and Tommy, his son, took me cat fishing. We caught so many huge fish under a meteor shower that they were hard to carry out. I tripped and cut my chin but denied stitches. My neighbors helped stop the bleeding. Barb and Shorty had became close friends and he took it hard when we parted. He was concerned about me now, as he had never seen me live so alone. Shorty needed and deserved to hear from me. Over the fence one night, I had to reassure him. I didn't say much, but I was absolute with my conviction.

"Shorty — I am not going down."

He was relieved to hear me say something. It was hard to say, but I was sure I was going to get up again. That was all that needed to be said.

My spirit grew during the empty year. Although I was far from a consistent walk with God, my path had fewer detours. I thanked God for what I had and for His forgiveness — and I made greater effort to seek His guidance. I became less willful because He broke me. Nevertheless, I didn't believe I could be a blessing to others. My ghosts were numerous and self-forgiveness came slowly. Too bull-headed to let the Lord take complete control, I did set sail in that direction. I was guilty as sin for so many things, but God offers mercy over justice and I kept trying.

My workouts focused on what it would take to water ski. It had been over two years since I topped the water. Getting bashed against concrete and receiving a permanent blow to a spinal cord isn't a yank on a hangnail. I needed over two years of nursing. It ran against the grain of my defiant nature for that much help to be necessary. An instinctive light came on in my head indicating that the time for nursing was over. I could cowboy up and ride away—and the fish would school again. As I always did when my actions were proper and common sense dictated, prayer guided the transition. God's control galvanized me.

Five ~ Schooling

Making the Cut

It felt strange for a common laborer to approach the day with such confidence. I wasn't applying to wash dishes though and upgrading my social status seemed a real possibility that I could taste. The College of Health steps were too steep to climb on a cane but I eased up and went inside. My entry interview into the School of Occupational Therapy would determine if I was the man for the job. The Student Search Committee was gracious to talk to me. Chaired by Professor Sharon Sanderson, the Assistant Dean of Student Affairs, the committee selected a few from the lot. I had a chance.

Prof. Sanderson, OT professors, and student members of the committee took notes. I was taken by how smart and pretty the young students were. I found it odd that I thought this, but it was hard to deny. I hadn't been out since Barb and I split. I accepted my reaction as natural and did not let it distract me much.

The questions were fair and I was comfortable.

"What made you want to enter the field of Occupational Therapy?"

I explained how I got hurt and underwent rehab—and shared the OT Chief's suggestion that I try to join them.

"How will your impairment affect the patients you treat?"

I hadn't considered it. "I hope the patients identify with my success and will recover with my help." I felt good when I spoke.

They asked how I would afford to get through college and I shared my story. We talked for a while and their pencils kept moving. Nobody threw their notes in the trash, or left early, so I guessed it went well. The search committee knew I wasn't their typical Junior Leaguer. I hoped that my rough edges would not eliminate me. Later they honored me by extending an invitation. I would start in the fall semester as an incoming member of the Junior Class of Occupational Therapy.

As the summer breeze began to cool and the talk of football filled the air, I prepared to enter the OT program. I was in tip-top shape. Despite everything that had gone down, sanity crept back into my head. My positive mood opened the next chapter of my ever-changing life.

Not Kansas Anymore

The OT senior class invited the incoming junior class to orientation. I didn't know what to expect. Forty young women joined three guys. To the old Hodge it was a place to find bed partners, but now I got hyper stimulated and overwhelmed. My fear of crowds gnawed away. After I could breathe, the scene again looked like a target rich environment. Lust overtakes a man. I wasn't at ease and felt like a porcupine in a balloon display. A blindfolded soul strapped to a post in front of a firing squad would feel more comfortable.

We played a game to relax new students and provide introductions. This activity paired those who lived near by so they could carpool. The mood was hysterical in the gathering dominated by females. My target impression caved in this unfamiliar setting that featured no traditional male teddy bears like a keg or pool table. I flopped around gasping for air. The seniors told us to park four blocks south. We walked through the classrooms, labs and lecture halls. Everyone ate next door in a small lunchroom. There would be few chances to eat once school started.

Appearing calm as I milled around, I felt like I had swallowed a nuclear warhead. Shelled up and sick with inadequacy, I didn't learn a single female by name. Only two other guys were there and I knew their names. My classmate Roger seemed nice but weird. Disgusted by the whole event, I guessed my fleshy side ruined it—but no familiar ruler was handy to measure what occurred.

My biggest challenge each morning was trying to get from parking lot "D" to the basement bathroom at the college which required me to ambulate four blocks, descend down one ramp and open three doors. I could count every step and I liked the exercise so I chose not to get a handicapped parking card. With a tired body and a spastic bladder and bowel that were not in complete control, the journey from "D" lot could be hazardous. External catheters failed with my high level of activity. At times, mishaps occurred. I didn't say anything and backpacked items to clean up.

Dr. Kathlyn Reed taught statistics class. Roger arrived late one day and didn't notice that the lecture had started. He stood in front of me and said, "Good morning, Hodge. Try some of this water." He opened his Mason jar to pour me a cup.

Roger danced to his own drummer who couldn't keep time. Possessing a kind heart but with no situational awareness, he stepped deep in doo-doo as a habit. Seemingly unaware of the scene created by his rude interruption, I cued him. "Thanks, Roger. Sit down. Dr. Reed is teaching."

He turned and greeted our professor. "Good morning, Dr. Reed! My apologies!" Roger seated himself, oblivious to his bizarre behavior. He wasn't on drugs, but maybe needed to be.

Dr. Reed stared at him as did everyone else and continued her presentation to our incoming class of eighteen. Dr. Reed was smart as a whip, well versed in the history of OT, but she was not a powder keg of excitement.

It was a grand challenge staying awake in Dr. Reed's class. One day I dozed off and leaned over my desk fender. My tongue was about to touch the ground in a small puddle of drool, when Dr. Reed asked me a question. I awoke and answered. Class ended and

Hodge Wood

I found my way through the sleep fog outside of the classroom. I was gang hugged in the hall by my classmates. They were amused to view my consciousness return and correctly answer Dr. Reed. The girls had a ball describing what they saw. I didn't mean to doze off—she was the OT Department Head. Dr. Reed was surprised to see that I studied at home and made an A in her class.

Roger voiced interest in Far East meditation and said he owned the latest herbal-based cure-all. If he didn't have a girlfriend, Kathleen, I would have bet he was gay. Being the only guys in class, we tended to visit more. Roger was way too strange. He invited me over. I qualified that Kathleen was going to be there.

Roger was one of many in health care who knew that he could cure me. He showed me the natural potions he had at home that would mend my paralysis. He thought he could make me able to run the forty-yard dash in record time—I'd be in perfect neurological health. His heart was pure. At Roger's direction, I found myself sitting under a black light in my underwear wearing green goggles. I had to leave and then distanced myself from him. He got behind and didn't graduate with our class but later developed an OT practice that matched his far out, snake oil salesman personality.

I developed the right way to work with my female classmates, but men are different from women. Primitive codes in my chemistry delivered lusty ideas and it was a constant battle to maintain control. All during class, natural thoughts ran through my testosterone-infested mind.

I looked around the classroom. The quiet girl had a distinct attraction, but she was in a close race in a large heap. Her Arabian eyes killed me, her smile seduced and her body was petite and firm—as I liked them. The tall blonde came to me to share her opinions. She had distinct features like a supermodel. Her attorney boyfriend might screw up and lose her, she warned. The voluptuous blonde liked to talk about sex and drink alcohol, so we had a lot in common. She gave my hanky-panky brain a lot to imagine. Our outstanding Christian in the bunch might not fall into moral failure, but she was too cute to not be suspect. The list continued. The best part was that my class of females would flirt and dare you to flirt back. The worst part was that we stayed busier than hell and had little time to create mischief. It was rare to get together one-on-one and then it was in study hall. Our labs were physical and we had to learn to touch to assess muscle tone, strength, reflexes and the gamut. Our junior class parties ended and we were back to schoolwork. I sensed an unwritten rule. We were to be involved for two years of study and should be careful. Chances arose to fandango with my classmates, but it was taboo. I swam around with students in other fields of study and hoped to find fish that liked my spots in those blue waters.

Our courses covered the life span that started before birth. Trying to keep it all sponged up for use was a trick. We learned movement sequence and primitive reflexes. Tests proved how much we didn't know. These eye openers made us humble and created a desire to learn to become future therapists. We identified muscles, their attachments, nerve innervations, ligaments and tendons. We learned how to evaluate for pathology from injury or illness. Class members acquired the skill to isolate, range and exercise muscle groups. We built and fit splints. The instructors showed body parts "in situ"—in their full and natural setting. Every day brought heaps of new information.

Students from all disciplines met for Dr. Mike Ferguson's pathology class in the grand auditorium. Stadium seating ramped down to Mike and the largest screen and chalkboard I had ever seen. He had the latest technology and knew so much. Professor Mike wore a white lab coat. He needed a haircut and if you didn't know him, he looked unimpressive. People took advantage of him and it made me angry. I knew his heart. He loved it when students learned and he stayed from four in the morning to dark. He taught the most difficult courses—anatomy and neuroanatomy. Both required his leadership within lecture and lab.

One day in pathology class, Mike covered new diseases discovered within the multitude of existing ones. He showed what they looked like through a microscope on the big board. Mike described each disease's cause, effect, treatments and hazards. He put up a slide and amazed me when he spoke. "This is a blood borne pathogen that will soon be recognized as a major killer. It is an HI virus and presents a condition known as Auto Immune Deficiency Syndrome . . . AIDS for short." Mike elaborated about AIDS through detailed studies—and then returned to the theme of his message. "This condition is sexually transmitted through homosexual contact and then through secondary blood transfusion and heterosexual sex with an infected partner. There is no cure. Trust me—AIDS will kill a lot of people."

We had never heard of it.

Lab Orientation

The sign on the locked door to the anatomy lab on fourth floor read, "No Admission Without Clearance." Mike released the latch and made the door alarm go off so we could hear it before introducing us to Marge, our other instructor.

We walked in. The six steel tables with large buckets underneath refracted sunlight from the windows and glared into my eyes. The bodies covered with plastic sheets smelled of formaldehyde. The strong odor took our breath. We were in a brand new world.

Marge defined Anatomy as "the science of the structure of the animal body and the relations of its various parts." They placed us in groups at tables. We were required to dissect the specimens and to teach each other. Marge said to work fast and not talk unless it related. She gave housekeeping orders—wear plastic gloves and lab coats, report scalpel wounds—and put all "unused fascia" in the buckets to avoid a slip hazard. The teachers described exactly what we should and shouldn't do. It was a strict new world.

Marge instructed, "Specific anatomy will be prepared, tagged and hung from the ceiling for testing purposes. Views on opened cadavers will also be prepared and tagged." It sounded like a freak show and I was in it.

Mike added, "Everyone will need to identify the cause of death from each table. It is easy at times with the removal of a black cancerous lung or a gunshot wound. Other times will be more difficult." He showed us the tools we would use. "Here is an electric bone saw for cutting the brain box." Things were easy to say. The professors in our new world were just having another day.

Mike said that the first cadaver was face down to condition us. He uncovered a naked male that had yellowed. The odor grew.

"Are there any questions?" Mike asked.

I had at least a million but preferred not to ask them.

After a pause, a female OT buddy chuckled and asked, "Will we dissect the penis?"

The girls thought that question was a hoot. I joined in with an insincere laugh.

Mike gave a quick reply. "Yes, the penis will be transversely cross-sectioned and longitudinally dissected with all structures progressively removed and identified down to the internal urethra." He added, "All students will find the pelvic anatomy quite interesting, but difficult for dissection as there are no square grid formations to use as landmarks, such as found in the thorax. The vagina and related genitalia dissections are some of the most fascinating structures to dissect." He concluded, "In this lab you get to see and feel the reproductive systems of male and female, 'in situ.'"

That was all we cared to know for the first day.

Fishing Around

I missed boating and kept my plans to ski again. I found my first boat for $1500—a discontinued Wonderglas. It was late season and many boats were for sale. I could not afford any of them so the bank loaned me the money. A sixteen-footer with a sixty-five HP Evinrude, it could run at thirty-two miles per hour. The seats folded down flat and I crawled into the parked boat at night to watch the stars. I bought some skis and an inner tube that I could ride if someone would pull me. I headed in the right direction for oxygenated water and fertile breeding grounds.

If I could squeeze in a lake run, the Draper Lake launch ramp was ten miles away. Life was looking good. I spent most of my time in classes with up to a hundred females. Chances were high that some of the young women might want to put on their bikini and go to the lake with me before it turned cold. Good navigation plan, I was sure. My gills were bright red, but I hadn't dated anyone.

I pulled the trigger on a date plan and sat next to a pretty blonde in pathology. I had seen her before in class. For me to ask anybody out was as simple as strapping myself into an electric chair and hitting the switch. The pretty blonde and I took notes from Mike's lecture. My mind wandered and I think she knew it. Instincts lead me to believe she might be thinking like me.

With Medal of Honor courage, I spoke at the end of the lecture. "What are you studying to be?"

She smiled as we caught eyes and didn't seem to be in a hurry to leave. "Radiology—and I work full time."

"Are you doing okay with work and school?"

"A's, but I work nights and never sleep. Makes it real hard to party."

I did some quick thinking. College students don't sleep. I did. If I didn't, my extremities burned worse, walking was harder and I peed all over myself. I hadn't partied but was game. My blonde classmate was interested in talking, willing to outline her schedule and liked to party. Like the rest of us, she had little time. I knew urgency faced me to get a date. Now was the time to ask but my confidence was shaky. "Would you like to go out? I've got a ski boat and can pull you . . . but don't feel obligated."

"Sure," she said and reached for a note pad. "Here is my number—what is your name?"

"Hodge. What's yours?"

"Barbara," she said. She turned away to vacate the desk.

"Barbara?" My eyes crossed and my brain rattled. I followed Barbara down the aisle and watched her behind. She waved goodbye and I said, "See you later." It took effort. Her note spelled out her full name, with a happy face that said "thanks!" The luck of the draw—her name was Barbara. That added complexity to my plan.

My old truck was a gas-guzzler. School was ten miles from where I lived. To save money, I considered buying a motorcycle so I stopped by the cycle shop to look for one. It took lots of denial and stupidity to go in but I had plenty of both. My severe impairment made riding a motorcycle as dangerous as jumping in front of a freight train.

The nervous salesman helped me raise my left leg over a cycle seat. I wobbled on my right one. I could keep it upright from the kickstand, but shook thinking about how I would perform on the road. I couldn't hit the right hand or foot brake, or react to catch my balance, due to the paralysis. The salesman had to help me off. I felt like a stooge.

He understood I wanted to save money, a motorcycle was out and a small car wasn't affordable. He shared an idea. "Would you like a safe new machine to ride to school that gets over fifty miles to the gallon and only costs three hundred bucks?"

Hodge Wood

I test-drove a step-through Honda 40 CC scooter in the parking lot. "How do I keep from being seen?" I asked.

He closed me. "It's brand new, looks good and you've got a basket for your books. Park it close—no walking from D lot." He followed me home in my pick up. I was learning to adapt in leaps and bounds.

Barbara was a likable person with a great memory for school material. She could work and study for two days at a stretch without sleep, test without review and made A's. A hard worker, she earned her keep and didn't expect anything from anyone. With her impressive lifestyle that contrasted with the rich kids at college, we had a lot in common and enjoyed dating. At the lake, she skied and pulled me on the tube. After getting naked together a couple of times, few sparks flew. We shared no sustained attraction, so we naturally swam in different directions. Starting the dating process again got more than my feet wet, but something was missing.

I switched my attention to an unnamed voluptuous OT classmate—and we found ourselves at the lake one day. She was a happy spirit and an eye catcher. Her cute little body spilled out of her strap bikini. We were having a blast and both of us felt the right lustful chemistry. The inner tube tossed me off undertow. She parked the boat next to me and jumped out in the water.

"I didn't know if you were okay," she said as she laughed and rubbed against me.

We splashed around with our bodies together. She was a looker and a friend. We touched and turned on, daring one another. However, I hesitated.

We went back to my place. Far too many shots of tequila later, I sensed it was time to move in on her bikini-clad body—but also sensed I shouldn't. My voluptuous friend wanted to fish—not just cut bait, but I didn't want to take it any further sexually. A kiss good-bye on the forehead shocked her. I slept after she left—and felt good doing it.

I had been back through the dating ritual but couldn't continue. I wanted for more. One night, I sensed a close presence of God. I had not been unloved in life—quite the contrary. More college women were available than I ever wished for and without obligation, but my spirit didn't want it that way. My relationships had fallen short. I wanted one God-sent person. In a spiritual realm, it was time to be accountable to someone who would benefit from my continued companionship. I could wait.

This night, I had faith that God had that special person for me. I had been impulsive, paid consequences and caused sorrow. God had not led and it had been rough. On my knees I prayed, asking Him to bring that special person into my life and that I be all she imagined. I awoke, refreshed in spirit and empowered by a peace of mind. God would guard and guide my heart.

Healing Power

I never missed a football game at the university. As a rule, the Sooner football team finished in the top three during the seventies. Heisman Trophy winner Billy Sims returned in 1979. For the second year, he led the nation in rushing. Sims reversed directions on a dime and stiff-armed a defender's head into his neck. Future Congressman JC Watts quarterbacked the wishbone to perfection. The "Ministers of Defense" were on the other side of the ball. Head coach Barry Switzer was the "King." He took over the program in 1973 under probation and won National Championships in 1974 and 1975. Sooner football had a healing power.

Switzer used charm and charisma. He injected emotions into players and motivated them to perform like Kamikaze pilots. Switzer described the game in a way nobody could. Down home and shooting from the hip, he said what he thought. It bent a few people out of shape. One day, as Barry walked out onto the field, a reporter asked how the team would perform. He looked up and gave a classic answer. "Clear blue sky and a dry field—we'll hang half a hundred on them."

They did.

OU football looked magical. My student section ticket was a priceless possession. Stair climbing on a cane couldn't stop me and I chanced a fall to watch the "Sooner Magic" with the faithful. It was a cultural experience on a fall Saturday afternoon. This year we often cheered for the Crimson and Cream in a track meet—a term first defined by Coach Switzer and later used by everyone. Going to the games healed me. I was in love with life and a major part of my life was Sooner football.

Out of My League

My left handwriting skills were slow, so I borrowed notes. Deb Swenson was my friend and best contact. Her notes were thorough and legible—and she liked to help. If I asked to borrow notes from others and got strange vibes, I didn't ask again. Those responses were tough to analyze, but I chalked it up to competition.

The copy window opened at lunchtime. Everyone rushed to get copies, but I had two speeds to get anywhere—stop and go. The end of the copy line was okay—the more time, the better. An OT senior named Beth Case ran the machine to make a few bucks during her lunch break. A wait in line watching Beth made my day. She infatuated me, but I would not dare say so. I savored the time that I got to stand in line while students hustled between classes to have Beth copy for them.

Beth was short and cute, with long brown hair that touched her hips. She helped the rude and polite the same way, with a glowing smile that melted me. Her speech was articulate—and I could tell she came from somewhere other than Oklahoma. She had kiss-me lips and a cheerleader's body. With or without make-up, she gave me a hormonal rush. I hoped to be inconspicuous, but I couldn't take my eyes off of her. She wore no trendy things. A homemade seashell belt accentuated her slender abdomen. I begged myself not to touch. Her perfume was distinct. When Beth leaned over the copy machine, I gawked at her butt. I thought she would catch me.

Beth scrambled to make my copies and I joked with her. "Hey Beth—are you just being lazy again today?"

She would laugh and reply. "No. Fine. Just busy."

Her response had nothing to do with my flirting comments. I suspected she couldn't hear over the copy machine. It didn't matter. I loved to hear her voice.

I thought every day about asking her out. I didn't. She was on my mind all the time. Infatuation is interesting, but Beth was way out of my league.

Cadaver Lives

I dissected the heart out of the cadaver in anatomy lab at our table and had my Crafts textbook out to learn more. I held the heart in my left hand, leaned onto my right elbow and studied my text. My assignment included teaching my lab mates about the heart and I was preparing to do a thorough job.

Classmate Linda stuck her boobs under my nose. She flashed a naughty smile and asked, "What are you looking at?"

I studied her breasts. "Linda cut it out. You kill me when you do that. I'm gonna spank you."

She ducked back to her table. Her comedy tickled me. Goofiness gassed in at that point, I guessed.

Dave was my pre-med buddy working at the next table. His group had sawed off the top of the brain box and had removed the brain from their cadaver. They were close to finishing with facial dissection and both eye orbits were empty. Dave got my attention in a peculiar way. He need not gain Mike or Marge's attention from across the room or they might kill him for his antics but he knew I would see the humor in his deviant behavior. Dave reached under the remaining skull, placed his hand through the opening and slid his hand up into the skull. Just as he did that, he alerted me.

Dave stuck two of his fingers through the empty eye orbits, raised the skull up at me and shook it as he wiggled his fingers. He let go of a "Hooo - Hooo - Hooooo!" sound and removed his hand.

I bit my tongue and laughed until I had tears in my eyes. Dave had brought one of our cadavers back to life. This was morbid and danged funny. I guess we were all acclimated to the anatomy lab as the endless hours we spent there marched on.

Last Ride

Michael P's familiar voice sounded on the other end of the phone. "Hey man."

"How's it goin'?"

"Cool. Ya' there?"

"Yeah—studying."

"Be right over—got somethin'."

I needed a break. The fall evening air was still warm and it breezed through my living room. Walter peered through bloodshot eyes over the aluminum kick panel on the back door and I went to pet him before returning to study the heart. I read how the superior vena cava starts by union of the brachiocephalics at the level of the first right costal cartilage. We were to have a major anatomy exam—and I felt prepared.

Loud pipes announced the arrival of the Harley Davidson as Michael P pulled into the front yard. Large ape hangers and suicide pegs were visible on the sleek black cycle in the dark when I stepped out onto the porch. Michael P, dressed in leathers, cranked the throttle a couple of times to reverberate the pipes.

Michael spoke. "Got another Sportster. Wanna ride?"

"Yeah, come in and let me get on some clothes."

I selected an album, handed the cover to Michael P and placed the record on. The song, "Doolin-Dalton," overtook my emotions.

Before getting hurt, I was a melody and chord player—a fake guitarist. I enjoyed playing, but now my paralyzed hands set me back. My left ring and little finger weren't able to hit frets. I couldn't hold a pick in my right hand. I described this to Michael P and he nodded that he understood. His simple responses were enough to help me. We listened to the Eagles over a couple of beers then I changed clothes and we hit the road.

I hadn't ridden since before I broke my neck. I hollered to Michael over the pipes. "My right foot is catching bumps and trying to spasm right off the peg!"

He yelled, "Can you hold on?"

"Yeah—holding on with my legs—they're weak. Don't turn fast!"

He wasn't reckless, but after getting on, I wasn't sure I wanted to stay. We drove to Lake Thunderbird, had a beer and headed back. It was all I could do to balance and keep my foot from falling. When I got off at home, I couldn't walk. It was my last ride.

Don't Wake Me

I was in study hall in the basement of the college one morning with two females. My eyes caught Stephanie's as she walked by. She was a senior OT student. Out of the blue, my lips moved. "Stephanie if you see Beth Case, please tell her I want to talk."

I seldom spoke to Stephanie and she appeared dumbfounded. She acknowledged that she would relate the message and passed on through.

In less than five minutes, I looked into Beth Case's happy face and she asked me the inevitable. "Did you want to talk to me?"

My hair-triggered brain wanted to ask Beth out and I had popped off to Stephanie without thinking. I could not believe I had pulled the switch on the thought of talking to Beth Case about going out. I looked into Beth's gorgeous eyes and realized that I was unprepared to ask her out—and had an audience to watch me flounder doing it. Time seemed to stand still and my throat felt like I had halfway swallowed a hardball. Somehow I managed to speak. "Hi, Beth—I was wondering—would you like to go to the football game Saturday?"

My mouth was desert dry and I felt my tongue sticking to my gums when I formed words. My lips had super glue applied. My heart thumped so hard and fast I was sure Beth could hear it. If the building had caught on fire, I would have been unable to stand up to walk out.

Beth responded. "Just a minute. Let me look."

Beth reached to get her black book out. I just knew entries stuffed it full of dates with rich, young handsome men. She checked her schedule.

"Okay, sure," she said.

It was a miracle. Her schedule had an opening. Numb, I was still able to get Beth's number and address. She lived within two miles of my house. I called Michael P to say I had a date with the prettiest girl at the University of Oklahoma.

Before our date, Beth caught me pulling up to the front of the College of Health on my step-through scooter. I felt like a bozo on the little rice burner. We visited and she left. She had no problem with the circus clown machine or me.

Game day was sunny and cool. I felt good. I pulled my truck into Beth's driveway and stepped to the door. She met me and we headed to watch football. Beth looked fine in my truck. We talked about many things. Beth moved from North Carolina where basketball was supreme. I told her about watching the Tar Heels play football while I was in a wheelchair. She heard the junior class had an incoming quadriplegic and was surprised to see me walking. Her interest was genuine and I was comfortable telling my story. We were at ease, considering the eagerness in the air.

We approached the entries under Memorial Stadium and Beth walked towards another ramp. It puzzled me and I spoke. "Aren't you going to sit with me?"

She turned back and looked relieved. "Oh, yes, just a minute. I have to go to the rest room." Beth ran to the women's room and she blended in with the other 75,000 people in red.

"Hmmm, she was heading for another gate," I thought. I kept my eyes peeled and she returned with bright red lipstick on that she wasn't wearing when she left.

Words came easy. "You are pretty, Beth. What kind of perfume is that?"

She blushed and smiled eye to eye. "Enjoli . . . Thank you, Hodge."

I knew now. The sweet perfume I smelled each day at the copy office was Enjoli. We sat close at the football game. I was love struck. If time stood still, I would have been pleased. My feelings were like junior high again. I hoped nobody would wake me from this dream. Other OT classmates gathered above the band in the student section. There was some concern over the class dating taboo. Most were delighted. Whatever others thought or felt didn't matter. I knew that Beth and I were off to a great start.

The Sooners played their usual game, with gang tackles and gazelles running the football. The Sooner Schooner raced across the green turf pulled by ponies Boomer and Sooner. We yelled, "Run those ponies!" We clapped as the band played "Boomer Sooner." Each time the wishbone lined up, we expected a score. JC Watts slid down the line to hand off to Billy Sims and he pummeled through gaping holes. The game went our way. We believed. Positive things happened on the field. Sooner Magic was on display.

Intuition revealed magic at work on Beth and me. During the game, it was too loud to talk much. Our sensuous eye contact kept speaking. Beth was fine with assisting me on the stairs. Her presence helped me overcome fears and relax. I had not relaxed for a long time. I felt wonderful.

After the game, I hoped to take Beth over to Michael P's ranch house. His large home was comfortable and it was just a short drive across Norman. He was a Sooner Football addict and would be getting in from the game. Everybody had a good time with Michael P—and Beth would too. I asked her.

She said, "You bet! Let's go!" Her enthusiasm astonished me.

Beth sat closer in the truck. I was happy to be with her and said so. I felt ten feet tall. I was excited, yet comfortable which was a surprise. Everything else was icing on the cake.

Michael P's windows were open in the pleasant weather. Out front we could hear Santana's "Love, Devotion and Surrender" playing through the stereo. We entered and his tape made an easy transition to the Beatles' "Strawberry Fields." The mood was nice and smooth which was normal at his place. He was out. As Beth milled around and looked over Michael P's decor, I gazed at her.

Michael P entered from the back room. "Hello, Beth, I am Michael P. So good to meet you. Hodge spoke highly of you. Can I get you a beer?" He was cordial with everyone and it made me feel good for Beth to feel welcome.

"Thanks!" She gestured a warm greeting with a smile.

Beth and I parked on the pit couch and Michael P added a humorous comment. "Hodge, I will go to the bar and buy you a beer, too, okay?" He was already getting our brews.

Michael P came back and the three of us talked, laughed and relaxed. He described our colorful past. After a while, Michael P excused himself. His exit allowed privacy.

Beth and I seemed to know each another and it felt like we had been together. Lightning struck. We laughed, poked at each other and made eyes. We moved around from place to place and the relocating gave me different views. My infatuation worsened. Michael made brief entries to change the music or to check if we needed anything. We were fine.

My melon head didn't remember her from the junior class orientation and it hurt her feelings. She was the classmate who lived within two miles of my house and she had hoped to carpool after telling me that. I reflected on my brain failure during the occasion and opened up about that day. Beth understood. She hinted that she had had a crush on me from the start, but during orientation, I hadn't paid any attention to her. How wild!

I described how I felt about her. "I figured you knew I was stalking you at the copy office window."

She didn't.

During a bathroom break I prayed that I wouldn't say or do anything wrong—and went back to the couch. Beth told me she couldn't believe I hadn't asked her out. She hoped I would. I told her how I forced myself not to ask, fearful of rejection. I described how I felt when I did it.

"I thought your black book was full of dates."

"My black book has my babysitting schedule. I don't get asked out much."

We cackled.

"I have one other date planned with a dentist," Beth said.

"Would you consider canceling?"

I had one other date set, but after the day was over, I called it off without telling Beth. She canceled hers with the dentist, but I didn't know until later. We never dated anybody else.

On the way home I learned Beth's mom and dad had moved to Oklahoma for business reasons. She had a microbiology scholarship at Duke, but the move eliminated her. She was out of state on the paperwork. She cried as they moved west and the trees grew shorter. Beth rode a bicycle on the main campus in Norman, lived in the dorm and waited tables at the pub next to the football stadium before getting into the OT program. She paid her way through school and moved back in with her folks to save money when she transferred to the College of Health. Her parents sometimes loaned her an older Oldsmobile to drive to school, but her mother brought her most of the time. They needed the car and their tractor firm was not far from the college.

"Would you like to carpool to school Monday?" I asked.

She appreciated it.

Beth had two OT internships after the first of the year. She had one in physical disability at Oklahoma Memorial Hospital before going to her final three month psychiatric rotation in Chapel Hill, North Carolina. She would graduate and take her registration examination to gain an OTR credential. We pulled up to her parents' house and came up for air with the same thoughts . . . Could we believe it? It feels real!

Going to the door, I was curious if Beth would mind letting me sleep on the porch. I said, "Beth, I had the best time that I could imagine."

"Me, too—thanks." Her sincerity built confidence.

We kissed.

I asked, "Can I call you?"

Beth smiled. "I hope so."

I gassed up the truck and ditched the step-through scooter. We were beyond carpooling.

Back to Blue Water

The long lab sessions put my standing stamina to a test. I directed my exercises at developing strength to last through them.

Chum Water

I had moved my workouts to the Health Spa. My spinal cord injury raised concerns for the guys in charge, but I had talked them into letting me join. The change to the spa provided me with flexible hours and the company of younger people. Everyone noticed my movement deficits, the different routine that I used and the brace and cane. The regulars were power lifters. They picked up on what I was accomplishing and accepted me as one of their own.

My weight returned to the same as before paralysis, but with only one-fourth as much strength on my right side. Left side strength compared more favorably to pre-injury level, but remained weaker. Bilateral lifting didn't measure up due to imbalance. Bicep muscles were the same as before injury, but I couldn't curl as much weight because my right hand couldn't grasp well. Velcro kept my hand tight around the curl bar.

I saw an improving body in the spa mirror, but it was one with permanent damage. My waist remained large with no grid. I wasn't fat, I just didn't have a good cut. My chest was smaller and I had little motion in my right chest wall. I would never jump up to kick the door frame above my head again. After taking Beth out, I had a primary reason to be inspired. From the beginning to the end of every day, my mind was on her.

One day, we didn't carpool and I asked Beth to rendezvous and go to our watering hole. I waited in D lot next to "Old Blue," the name we had given her Olds. She showed up and we rode to Triples in my truck.

We sat across from each other in a secluded booth. We got loose on Tequila Sunrises and it was coincidental that we both had spare time. With our shoes slipped off under the table, we rubbed feet against legs. Our eyes remained connected. We held hands and talked. Our relationship moved way too fast for both of us. We had fallen in love. When flames leap around, you notice the heat.

Beth informed me of a concern. "My Memorial Hospital rotation got canceled. I've been assigned to the VA here in the city."

It was regrettable. I said, "At least you will be here."

Beth had an option. "I could go to Muskogee but can't afford an apartment."

"Sorry you lost Memorial . . . I don't want you to go to Muskogee."

My words revealed possession and the peyote god allowed me to speak my heart. When my tequila-lubricated tongue made this intimate statement, two things came to mind. I had no right to possess Beth. We had been together for just a few weeks.

Beth asked, "Do you feel that way already?"

"Yes. I am surprised but I do."

As usual, I was way ahead of myself. But I thought and felt different than I ever had. I asked Beth from the gut, glad that we were alone and close. "How about you, Beth?"

She smiled and her eyes misted up. "Let's not do anything that we shouldn't do."

Beth didn't answer my question but gave good advice. Her VA rotation was important. I lightened the conversation and gave her plenty of room. We continued to lust on each other in the little booth, suspended from the crowd and away from all other responsibility. Beth gained confidence from our spiritual closeness. We held hands and shared loving eyes—at times without words.

The waitress eased up to our booth space. In a pleasant tone she asked, "Two more Tequila Sunrises?"

She caught us. We laughed and agreed to have another round.

She walked away to get drinks. I commented to Beth that I could play "Tequila Sunrise" on my guitar. "Would you like to come over and hear me play?"

"Sounds like fun!"

Chum Water

We returned to D lot to get Old Blue. She followed me and I watched her in the rear view, careful not to lose her. All at once, "Mr. Spinal Injury Problem Number One" showed up. The urge to pee was immediate two blocks from my house. I couldn't pull over and explain to Beth that I needed to use my urinal. I didn't think I could back track to a gas station. Stepping out of the truck to jettison fuel was out of the question. My best chance was to get home. It was dark when we pulled in my drive. Beth walked in front. I unlocked the door as my bladder kicked off and peed down my leg. She didn't notice the puddle on the concrete step.

Inside the door, Beth looked puzzled when I said, "I'm going to get a quick shower and change. Make yourself at home."

I came back after changing clothes and explained what had happened. We laughed about the mishap as we described the thoughts and feelings it caused us. Since Beth didn't know my dilemma, she got worried I would rush from the shower with immediate plans that she wasn't ready for. Her comical re-enactment described what she felt and thought while sitting alone in the living room. As strange as it was, an enjoyable time evolved from an awkward moment and there was a peaceful calm in the air around us. I logged the facts and mis-perceptions into my "Journal of Life with Spinal Injury."

Beth and I rubbed Walter, joked about little things and carried on in an air of playfulness around the house. We walked out to see the boat that I had bought to ski behind, someday. Returning inside, we stopped for a wonderful embrace. Sparks were flying. We were thirsty and went into the kitchen for water. Another 300-degree kiss ignited. We sat down and I retrieved my guitar. I asked Beth to sing along with my butchered up imitations of Eagles' songs. I could play a few rough licks and used a mouth harp around my neck. Beth laughed when she tried to sing, sat back and listened to me. She was easy to entertain because she liked what she heard and it wasn't much. I was at my best—half-bad.

Nobody knows the exact nature of how the brain processes feelings and emotions. Somehow, I knew Beth was for me. Far too rapidly, I felt this way. Beth leaned towards me on the couch and reminded me of our emotions at the copy office. She reflected back to when I asked her out to the football game and how she assumed we were carpooling. Tears came and then she broke into laughter as I got her a Kleenex and wiped her eyes and held her close.

"Jeez, Beth," I exhaled. "If you only knew how I felt about you from the start at the copy window."

The day had worn me out and I wanted to lie down. With no further intentions than to lie close together and rest, I said, "I'm tired, Beth. Come stretch out on the bed with me." I nudged her that way.

"But Hodge, we shouldn't," she said as she walked.

"We won't do anything we don't want to do—I promise."

I was tired and intended for us to rest. We eased into my bedroom.

Spontaneous Thermodynamics

With my shoes off, I stretched out on my back. Beth cuddled up into my arm as if created to fit there. She shook away fear before melting into me. Her eyes were moist against my neck and I wanted her to feel secure. We relaxed and enjoyed the serenity. We lay still for the longest time. Beth had curves like a swan. Her Enjoli perfume intoxicated me, as did her breast against my side. The relationship between heat and other volatile forms of energy caused spontaneous combustion. The cosmic fire caused no alarm but it needed tending.

Beth felt better than imagined and the plan to rest vanished. I released my worries in exchange for the night moves. I saw lightning and could not stay put. Our chemistry perpetuated desires far beyond resting and neither of us could control what happened in the erogenous zone we entered.

We rolled face to face and her lips opened against mine. Kissing her was like climax — except I got to kiss with no end to the explosive pleasure. We advanced and made out intimately. We were sweating as my leg slipped in further between her legs. Her response invited more. My lips hit an erotic trigger behind her ear and Beth sighed in sensual gratification. She molded on top.

Carefully, erotically and intentionally, I helped her take off her top and she took my shirt from me. Naked from our waist up, we necked and petted and took time in the delightful moment. Beth's skin was softer than I had dreamed about — when I begged not to touch her at the copy window. Beth found what she wanted. She rose up to help me lower her slacks and panties below her knees and I saw her exposed body in the soft light. I kissed and touched everywhere. Her eyes dilated like a full moon.

"Make sure or we won't . . ." I managed to say.

Inviting my eyes and assistance without words, Beth shook off her clothes and joined me naked.

I felt obliged to tell her my limits. "Beth, I can't orgasm because of my injury — I can't get you pregnant."

She didn't believe it and captured me. We made love until our strength was gone.

I remained aroused. With our future in mind, I felt apologetic since I didn't climax and addressed the thoughts that hit me. "You see how my spinal injury affects us? Will you be okay with it?"

My spinal injury was no problem with Beth because she liked the benefits. Later, she was in no mood to leave but her mom and dad would worry. I kissed her goodnight and couldn't wait to call her the next day.

I pinched myself to be sure it was real. My infatuation had been by-passed by another miraculous thought. Beth was that God-sent person. This fish was happy to be on her hook. I woke up early the next morning and dialed the phone. I asked Beth, "Are you OK?"

Hodge Wood

"Oh, yes—but I was afraid you might not call—that would have killed me."

She was relieved and I was surprised she didn't know better. "Could we get together today?" I said, with hope in my inflection.

"Oh, yeah. I have to study, though," she said in a pleasing tone.

"You are perfect," I told her.

I heard her mom and dad in the background. "When do you want to get together?" she asked.

"How about for breakfast—I worked up quite an appetite last night."

Beth laughed and I imagined how she felt with her parents listening in. "Would you meet my parents when you come over?"

"I look forward to it."

"When are you coming?"

"Right now."

Get Back In Line

We went at a hectic pace in school. Days crushed together with too many assignments and our class burned rubber from place to place. We hustled to change into shorts, flew to kinesiology lab and performed muscle tests on one another.

We shuffled from treatment table to table, observing various evaluative techniques while referencing the text. Professor Paula instructed a female student to get on her back with her feet hanging down over the end of the table. Paula stated that she would show how to identify short hip flexor muscles. She instructed the student to bend her left leg and hold it against her chest while maintaining the right leg flat. Short right hip flexors wouldn't allow the right leg to remain against the table and the picture in our text revealed the same finding.

Chum Water

The student did as told. With a leg folded against her chest and the other out flat, two points were obvious. One—her right hip flexor was of normal length. Two—the posture opened the crotch of her shorts for full view of her genitalia. I looked away to see my female classmates watching me and smiling. I was embarrassed for our exposed student—and knew she was unaware.

My back bedroom was filled with large ivy and begonias from cuttings my mother had grown. I tended the plants and the area became my major study space. One afternoon, Beth charged into the room. She seemed mad but laughed as we kissed hello.

Beth gave me a wrist splint she had fabricated in lab and said, "Look at this positive intrinsic."

I examined the splint and noticed that it had a nice extension angle. "Looks good."

Tears welled up in her eyes and I wondered what I did. "Sorry," I said.

"What for?"

"I don't know—but whatever made you cry."

Beth hugged me while trying to laugh and explained. Paula wouldn't accept the splint because she thought the wrist angle was incorrect, but it wasn't. Paula asked Beth to adjust it and Beth asked her to remeasure. Paula got mad in front of everyone and told Beth to correct it and get back in line. Beth knew it was correct and just got back in line.

Beth said, "When Paula looked at the splint again, she passed it."

"No fooling?" I added, "You have to respect rank at all cost, huh?"

She was okay. I gave her a big hug and we agreed to go to Michael P's house after the big game Saturday.

Hooked On Love

Beth and I held together like epoxy. It was hard to believe. After the game at Michael P's, she and I slipped into the shower. With hot water spraying under bright lights, we cleaned and caressed every micro-inch. Slippery soap ran under our hands on naked exposures until the hot water ran out. I turned the knob off and we continued exploring one another while standing on the tile. We provoked carnal natures and demanded reciprocal actions. Moist steam rose up from our skin. The hot water tank reheated, so I turned the shower and Beth back on. Erotic pleasure had never been this ideal and we voiced it. We toweled down and while in bed, advanced our sexual relationship further than we had ever intended and beyond what either of us had ever experienced. The complete shared satisfaction was a gift.

Later, guilt overtook me in the darkness. I thought about how fast our relationship had progressed. My days before Beth haunted me. I was a man with a memory. I placed Beth on a pedestal the first times we interacted and I had controlled myself. Back then I knew she was way beyond my league. My willpower had faded and I let myself go because I knew that God had sent me a prize—a companion that was an answer to prayer. This was as real as it gets and right. Other questions came to mind. What if I tell her all about me and she gets scared away? Can I take it? I thought not, but knew I had to come clean.

I released Beth, rolled on my back and said a silent prayer. Staring into the dark, I said, "Beth, there are things you should know. It will be hard to tell and hear."

I reflected on failed relationships, admitted to having unresolved feelings and exposed my weaknesses. I dug out all the trash. For a moment I stopped talking and became fearful—Beth was too quiet in the darkness of the bedroom. I went on. "I am telling you because I very much care for you."

Beth saw I was genuine and liked my honesty. I could have made a sham of our decent relationship without the frank exposure. Beth opened up to me. She had one previous relationship with a young man in North Carolina but the affair went out of control her senior year of high school. When she moved west, distance created infrequent contact. They faced problems together, but remained attracted. She said no more of it her sophomore year at OU. She got hurt in her one shot and gave her best effort in a losing deal. I studied her pain and recognized her sincerity. Nothing we spoke about in the dark was superficial. We had connected.

Our commitment surfaced. We never had insight and openness before like what we shared now. We knew our past. With a blanket of security covering us, we locked into our future. The Angel of Mercy hovered. After a long, silent pause, I said what I felt.

"Beth, I love you."

I was comfortable and the words were timely. Beth rolled over to me.

"Hodge, I love you, too."

We remained crazy in love from then on.

The cold, harsh winter arrived, but Beth and I were happy campers. On snow days, we wrapped up all day in a blanket on the floor. We shopped and bought her new clothes and attended church. I cooked romantic meals. Beth encouraged me to grow a full beard and nicknamed me, "Wooly Man." I had her baby blue shirt embroidered above her left breast with her nickname, "Sugarbush." We necked in the college parking lot. Friends noted how happy we were. Old buddies tried to coerce her away. It was the best time of our life. Beth gave me what I asked her for at Christmas. In the middle of the day and by surprise, she appeared with nothing on except bright red lipstick and a matching red ribbon around her waist. I was the luckiest ape on the planet.

Hodge Wood

In the dead of winter, my hopes to water ski remained and the spirit led me to react. Although I could not ski on two, it somehow made sense to buy a Jobe slalom water ski. It was long, increasing the chance to get up. I sat the ski next to my bedroom-dressing chair as a motivator. My primary goal for over two years was to water ski again.

Beth saw the ski and asked a logical question. "Why did you buy it?"

I had confidence. "I will ski on it someday."

Beth smiled at the thought and voiced support. "I hope so, Wooly Man!"

Sharp Blade

Michael P phoned. "Hey man, bad news. Barbara overdosed and she's in the hospital. I knew you would want to know."

I hung up shocked. Memory banks opened that had been locked shut. I had not seen or heard from Barb since we said good-bye. I had mended as much as anyone does when they have gaping holes in their lives. Since then, denial buried our pleasurable and painful times deep in my mind. That she might have endangered her life cut like a sharp blade. Drawers in my mind reopened which should have remained closed. Mental compartments fell out and spilled memories of the gut-wrenching past when I was on two fast legs and a foolish course. Barbara was a wonderful soul whom I had helped and hurt. Our past resurfaced and guilt flooded over the outcome. My mind sifted through pleasant and forgettable memories. God knew I still cared about Barbara. I had to see her.

Without issue, Beth escorted me to the ICU. Jimmy was there with Barbara. She was not very coherent but would live. I never saw her again. All that I could do after leaving Barb in the hospital was pray for her. I made a habit of doing so.

Ordinary

Marge and Mike decorated the anatomy lab with hanging body parts as they said they would do when class started. No test pins were in place yet, so who knew what would be on the final exam. The parts provided a zillion questions. They planned to add more and re-arrange them. The lab was not gory. Everything had become ordinary.

I joined a small group of students late in the lab one afternoon. We wanted to increase our chances of passing the final. On table two under the hanging parts dispersed throughout the lab, Dave led us in further dissecting the chest. All cadavers lay opened for the semester test. Each exposed different areas of the body. We were not there long when two uniformed campus police came charging through the entry door. Apparently, we triggered a silent alarm. These guys were first time visitors.

The officers exhaled heavily. "What are you doing in here?" one asked before leaving the lab. The other officer waited to hear our answer but had to sit down.

"Studying"

Hodge Wood

The policeman that remained in the lab tried to stand and observe as we tarried. His act to perform as if everything was normal conflicted with his shaking knees and flushed color. Suddenly, we caught him falling and seated him again in a chair. Once the officer was able to leave, we escorted him back out with our apologies for setting off the alarm.

Rich

I entered the lake often to try to ski but couldn't for nearly three years. The Lake Draper water was frigid in March as my effort continued. Through repeated trials, I could place two skis on, but it exhausted me. Idling behind the boat for hours of failure, I tried to come up with two handles, which is easier for a beginner. My right hand would not hold on. I went back to a single handle. Ski gloves gave me a chance if I bunched the material on the right to further increase my grasp, but it gave way. I ripped several gloves out as I tried and failed to come up.

My old position of standing up on skis would no longer work. When the boat accelerated, my right toe fell and the ski dove. My leg tried to come out of the hip joint as the ski ran under me. I gained a little control of my right leg by placing that ski out in front when the boat started towing. However, my strength left before I could stand up on water. It tested my patience but I could see how to do it. At times, skiing seemed futile but I remained determined to overcome. I never made it out of the water.

The new Jobe ski next to my dressing chair waited patiently each day for me to return. I picked it up that night with tired arms and wiped dust from the rubber boot. The silver and black top plate didn't have a single ding, and the bright orange bottom shined into my eyes. Bought to motivate, it fascinated me and sent a signal to my brain to keep trying.

A late snow marked the beginning of spring. Beth and I stayed attached like Siamese twins. She had survived the dungeon at the VA on her physical disabilities rotation. With new summer clothes in hand and sporting a short haircut, Beth packed to leave for North Carolina. She looked dazzling in a blue business suit. I calmed her fears and hid mine.

Beth's perfumed letters saved me. I stored them together and re-read them. A day didn't pass that I didn't write. We had a true love and I had no desire to be tempted away, despite the possibilities. Around the intensity of our routines, we lived for the phone to ring and could not hang it up. If my "had to do" list could include doing something for Beth, then I did it for her.

In woodworking shop, the occupational therapy student learns to use wood as a treatment tool. I built an easel from oak for Beth. I sanded on it until I couldn't move. Professor Terry did not allow many power tools in place of manual work. We could experience the strength building benefit.

Beth painted as a hobby. The easel could hold the gigantic picture of us that I had enlarged. Lord knows where it would go—but my mind was in the right place and I was thinking big. When I showed the picture on the easel later to Beth, she asked, "Where will we put it?" She was right. The picture was too large to put anywhere in our little world.

At the health spa, I gave all. With everything to live for, the effort was showing. We juniors became the seniors. Students who had not dropped out performed clinic observations, got a political edge for future jobs and understood the big picture in health care delivery. We were salmon preparing to swim upstream.

I left to fly out to North Carolina for spring break. Seated in the aircraft to take-off, I glanced at my Health Spa logo across the chest of my new shirt and smiled like I had a mouth full of persimmons. I would land in Raleigh-Durham Airport. Beth would pick me up for a week that would be ecstasy. My excitement could be no greater, even if the plane crashed.

We de-planed into the terminal. My neck stretched a foot in a scan for Beth. My ears perked up at her voice.

"Hi, stranger. Want to go for a ride with me?"

We kissed and hugged. Her literal presence awed me and I inhaled the Enjoli radiating from her neck. We hooked arm in arm and headed out into the green countryside. I could cut the humidity with a knife and that made Beth's pheromone identity even more distinct to my olfactory system. Upon arrival, I was sure I could never leave.

We carried on in the car and pulled over to kiss. Beth's apartment on top of a tree-covered hilltop had a twin bed with plenty of room for both of us. Her roommate was gone.

Beth introduced me to her coworkers but had a hard time remembering their names. This was uncharacteristic for her. Back alone at her pad, Beth broke some news that helped me realize why she seemed so spacey. If God didn't help her talk and make me listen, my story would have ended and I might have flown back to Oklahoma—or the moon.

Shamefaced, Beth led out. "I did not know anything about it ahead of time—I didn't plan it—it just happened—I wish that it didn't but it did—and that will be the last time—and it should have never happened."

She was off to a terrible start and my mind imagined the worse.

I responded. "What happened?"

We were already at a fever pitch.

"Last night, Alton was here."

Alton was her old boyfriend and I was thinking about packing to leave.

"No, no," Beth pleaded, as she sensed I might jump out of the window. She clarified. "I mean he didn't stay here."

I decided I would give her two more seconds.

"Hodge, he just showed up and didn't stay."

I needed to qualify what happened between show up and leave —and spelled that out.

Beth spoke some tangibles. "Hodge, Alton and I never spent time together since I came here. I ran into him at the grocery. He must have followed me on my bus and just showed up! I asked him to leave and told him you would be here today—and asked him why he would just show up like that—NOTHING HAPPENED BETWEEN US—NOTHING!"

Now Beth had reached the heart of the matter in my mind.

"Honey, you mean he just showed up?" I asked, looking for reassurance.

"Yes and I couldn't sleep thinking what might have happened if he had come today while you were here."

"Simple, I would have killed him," I said to help bleed off some adrenaline. "Did he want to stay?"

"Yes. I asked him to leave—several times—and he did—said he would leave me alone and never come back. I told him how much I love you and how close we are and that it was already over between him and me and would stay that way."

Beth was out of air and I relaxed.

I went over my thoughts and asked, "You told him about me? US? He just showed up and won't ever come back? Nothing happened? Did you kiss?"

Beth replied yes to all my queries, except that they didn't kiss. The visit was a mistake. Loyalty was in our portfolio.

I hugged Beth and said I was sorry it happened to her and that it was behind us. She made me proud because she told him about our bond. I had an afterthought. "If he comes by again I will rip his head off." A buck in rut is territorial.

Hodge Wood

Beth and I had the time of our lives in North Carolina. The trees were of diverse phylum. The large hills were mountains to a flatlander like me. She introduced me to the Blue Ridge Parkway in the Appalachians. Hours became days. A week without obligation and away from all distractions, we made simple plans that turned out to be grand. Camping in such a scenic place was a highlight of our week-long furlough. We arrived before the summer season opened, perfectly alone, with no patrol. We lived our version of rich. Our wealth consisted of a pup tent, a camera, grill-cooked food, a few bottles of Asti and each other. It was worth millions.

Cock of the Walk

I got home to Oklahoma, where the heat melts your brain and shade is a luxury. Beth would return the fourth of July and it wouldn't be a day too early. One afternoon in the late day sun, alone at the lake, I stretched out under my boat top and reflected on the past. My mind went back to a time when I was on strong, fast legs. The memories were vivid.

At work one summer on top of my Pepsi-Cola Bottling Company route truck in the lot of a Skaggs Albertson Supermarket, I re-stacked and tied in wooden crates of empty glass bottles three layers high for the ride back to the plant. Handled hard and fast, the crates of bottles clattered together and stuck in their place.

The Skaggs location had a strange aura. It was the same parking lot where I gashed my head open and got stitches. At this store, I crushed the end of my thumb one Saturday, had to have surgery and almost lost my job because I missed a few days.

Chum Water

Pausing on top of my truck, I watched the summer heat roll up in gaseous waves from the pavement. Gazing across the parking lot at the pavement releasing heat like a charcoal grill caused me to smile. My other stops were finished and the day's work would end as soon as I tied together a few more cases of empties. I had already thrown all of them from the ground onto the top of the truck. Going back and forth around the crates on the narrow edge of the truck top, I pushed and pulled bottles that hadn't already fallen into their wooden crates. It required skill to work along the narrow roof edge while on the balls of your feet with your heels hanging out in mid-air. Late in the day and well over one hundred degrees, sweat had soaked through my blue Pepsi uniform, as well as my socks and leather work gloves. Not everybody could do this work, which I found enjoyable.

My sales figures were as good as any at the factory. The route drivers competed. We enjoyed the camaraderie after work in the sales office at the Pepsi plant and then went and drank a beer or two. This day was no different. I planned to go to the "Cock of the Walk" bar in uniform with the other guys for an ice cold one. After that, it was time to race my dirt bike for the evening. The "Cock of the Walk" still had quarter draws. The sign on the wall said they always would or close. I liked that dedication. The bar owners liked Red, their Pepsi route man, and they treated all of us drivers from the plant kindly.

Working on top of my truck, the thought of the "Cock of the Walk" refreshed me. The air conditioning would be cold. It would be fun to meet Red, Clyde and the other men to play pool, darts and dominoes and to listen to music.

I picked up the pace on top of my truck so as to finish faster. I stepped back and forth on the narrow outside edge of the top of the truck. Looking down at the ground below, I noted that the sole of my work boot had pulled loose from the upper leather. I thought, I've worn out another pair and will have to buy more.

I hugged the last case of empty bottles against my chest from the back of the roof, turned and walked down the narrow space lined knee high with glass. My eyes centered in on an outside bottle in the wooden crate. The pop bottle was broken upward into a jagged, sharp point. It had pierced through my leather glove when I reached around behind the crate to pick it up. I spotted no blood but knew I'd need another pair of gloves.

The jagged bottle sticking through my glove distracted me. I stepped off the top of the truck into space and began a rapid twelve-foot descent to the ground. In a split second, I threw the case at the pavement below and kept my upright position. I hoped to break the glass into a thousand pieces before I landed on it. I planned to cushion my fall with my legs, stay on my feet and not touch the ground with either hand. The remnants would cut me to shreds with a slight mistake. I did it. The bottles blew into pieces and the crate disintegrated.

I looked up at the top of the truck I had just been standing on and said, "Thanks God!" Without a scratch, I spoke out loud a second time. "Time for a beer at the 'Cock of the Walk!'"

At that, my mind returned to real time. I cringed at the flashback and felt lucky. Subconsciously, I held to the cleat of the boat and remembered walking along the top of the truck and falling off. My grip relaxed. I thought about how strong I once was. It was weird how I missed it. So much had changed.

Keep the Corks

Beth came back, got her OT certification and went to work at Presbyterian in the brain injury program for Dr. George Prigatano. The hospital was across from the college, so we got to see each other on a regular basis. On the second of July, I hotfooted around and prepared big plans. In the sun, the asphalt had a melted texture that took your shoe impression—or the bottom layers of flesh if you had no shoes. I headed for the place and person I had genetic coding for—a lake and Beth.

Chum Water

Beth and I were on Draper Lake in the Wonderglas and everything was right. I pulled Beth on slalom and watched her tanned body flex in the skimpy bikini. She carved the water as I had taught her. She was in love with life and me. She pulled me fast on the inner tube—reckless like I wanted. Between runs we swam and played. It was our time in the sun. Once towed out, we anchored to eat from the ice chest I had packed.

Beth watched me pull the first of two bottles of Asti from the depths of the ice.

"Want summ'a this bubbly, Sugarbush?"

"You bet."

I placed two champagne glasses from the ice chest in her hands and asked, "Kind of memorable glasses, don't you think?"

She said, "Let's keep these Asti corks and label them for this occasion."

"Gladly," I said.

We had Asti corks from many previous times and there was reason to continue the tradition. With poise, Beth sat the two champagne glasses down on top of the chest, imagining that we were in a class restaurant.

"I love you," she said as she wrapped her arms around my neck.

With the cork paper unraveled, I pointed the bottle facing upwind. "Think I can shoot this thing where it will come back into the boat?"

Beth giggled and said, "Land it back here!"

I aimed the escaping cork. Whop! The cork sounded into the air and fell in the nose of the boat. I asked her to grab it. She turned her back and I placed a small velour box down the front of my swim trunks. She returned and the bubbly I poured made a cold, fizzy cloud above the carbonation. I handed her a glass.

I asked, "A toast?"

"Okay, but to what?"

"To another glass of Asti — after we down these."

Beth laughed and we inhaled the fresh champagne as fast as the seltzer effect would allow. Coolness filled my throat. Several refills followed and I could hear an orchestra in the background. We shared romantic entertainment.

"Would you go to the bar and buy us another round, Beth?"

Beth refilled and asked, "Another toast?"

"Sure!"

We caught eyes and I let the Lord put the words on my tongue. "To a long, happy and healthy life together . . . Beth, will you marry me?"

I presented Beth her engagement ring from within the velour box I had stuffed in my trunks. She was as delighted and stunned as I had hoped. Beth took the ring box and gazed at the gold and diamond inlay. She turned to me with joy and tears, held me and then looked back into my eyes.

She piped out her reply. "Yes!" It was simple and sure.

Exhilarated, we let the moment last. We sipped our way through the rest of the champagne and watched the blazing sun set and leave a cool breeze. We decided to marry on December 26th, as I would be on break before therapy rotations and would have time. As the champagne went down, we talked of a promising, fulfilling future. We engaged for a lifetime.

We became the talk of the town in our spheres of social influence. I asked her dad for his daughter's hand, although I was a nervous wreck. Ruth was happy, but she embarrassed me with a comment to persuade Beth to stay.

Ruth said, "He picks 'em too good looking and they run off."

Beth adored Ruth and accepted her comparisons. As turbulent as life was, I never lacked confidence that Beth and I were right together. God had paired us up.

Intellectual Currents

I headed down the stretch. Neuroanatomy was the most difficult class. Everyone took it during the last semester and it flunked some of the best. The nut cutting reached a peak. The coffee pot perked late and early to help pick up the knowledge.

We stood together in the fourth floor anatomy lab again. Dr. Ferguson provided neuro lab orientation to the class that he would teach, grade and make or break. Standing was brutal on me, due to the spinal injury. I could stay in one place a short time before my neurologic control centers set off alarms to sit down or at least move around—but stationary standing was a requirement and the weakness bells and pain whistles went off in my brain. When I did move I was Jell-O.

Mike opened some steel cabinets to remove some jars and informed us, in his matter-of-fact way, how we would learn to dissect the brain. Mike pulled brains and portions of brains from the large containers. Pointing to areas of these brains that were unfamiliar to us, Dr. Ferguson identified disease and described illnesses that we didn't know yet. There was much to learn.

The professor spoke and made comments about brain and spinal injury permanence. Nonchalantly, Mike pulled an intact infant head from a jar. Covered in dark black hair, it rolled across the stainless steel table after he had released it. He continued searching for other tissue samples in the same jar. The head made an abrupt stop and stared at me. I came close to falling and felt nauseous. Mike made no reference to the infant head. He was attracted to another one of his brains and made comments I missed. Neuroanatomy was going to be a humdinger.

Beth and I hit the lake each evening we could to ski and tube. I continued to try to get up on skis without success. Beth could drive a boat and she tuned in as I tried to come up on skis and adapted her towing to help me. Despite our best team effort, I was not capable. While trying to favor my weak right grasp, I blew several more glove seams out—many on the first wear at ten bucks a pop. I bought new wet suits to extend the season.

The fall and winter months whizzed by and Beth's staff called us Mr. and Mrs. Go Fast. She and I were at work or school, the health spa or lake. Dr. Prigatano provided delicious food and premium liquors at his prestigious gatherings. His staff fit me into their intellectual crowd. I had swum a distance from the "Cock of the Walk" and "Filthy McNasty" beer bars I'd frequented in the seventies. Whether in the beer bar or the hospital banquet hall, you play the nonsense game the same way. I knew the differences well and doubted many others did. The watering holes in the Medical Center had distinct advantages. It's easier to leave a party in the hospital suite when the server suggests time is up than to run out of a dive chased by a bouncer with a baseball bat.

Late that year, I studied neuronal pathways by drawing them on large sheets of butcher paper. They looked like road maps. I hung the papers for study on the walls of my plant room. It was my own form of art turned to science. The butcher paper let me examine why and how the brain and cord integrated. There were endless brain and spinal functions to study—and many hit home in my new role as a transitioning occupational therapist. I learned so I could better understand my own incomplete spinal injury. I found why even the simple was complex. My spinal cord had significant damage and a wall full of butcher paper showed what happened. I followed neuro class lectures and references, tacked the butcher paper up and traced down the answers.

Why was I able to move in the first place? Why does one side of my body move better than the other? Since I have better motion in my left side, why does it remain numb? Why am I able to pull hair out of it without feeling? Why am I spastic? Why can't I stand in place for long? Answers to these questions were in the book and traceable on the butcher paper. I found the detail of my injury and learned why I had problems. It wasn't just for my personal benefit. I studied to serve others too.

My south-side street smarts were of no value as I learned about neurologic function. I punched in all of my smart tickets to absorb the material and it took a lot of butcher paper. A neurological explanation is available for anything we do or act on. It amazed me to be fortunate enough to study it all—and to be able to think it through to the point I could use it. The human being provides intrigue. The Good Lord created miracles within each of us.

Nice Church Wedding

Beth came into the house as I studied my butcher paper. After hugs and kisses, she sat down to talk. "Mom is being difficult with our wedding plans," she said with a sigh.

I saw no reason for problems. "What do you mean? We chose our invitations, Mona at the bakery wants to work out details with your mother and cater for free . . . we agreed to no alcohol at the church. What's there to be difficult about?"

"Well, most of those things Mom isn't sure about or wants to change," Beth said with dismay.

I worried my mother would get cut out. I said, "Mom is old and works hard at the bakery. She won't stand for not being able to cater our wedding. Mona does weddings at the Governor's mansion." I asked, "What's the beef?"

Beth looked confused and spoke that way. "Mom will talk to Mona, but she isn't sure. She might turn down the free catering because she feels that if it isn't done the way she wants it, she can't say anything."

Hell's bells. I could tell we were going to have fun putting on a wedding.

Beth had a finale. She said, "You won't believe this. Mom says that the scripture from the Bible that we chose for the invitations concerns her. It reads, 'your family will be my family and your God my God,' and she is afraid people will think we had other gods before getting married." Beth knew how ridiculous it sounded and her voice began to crack. "Mom just rambles and doesn't seem to agree to anything or make any decisions—and the photographer told me he didn't think he could work with her." Beth was disgusted and broke down. Huge raindrop sized tears spilled from her eyes. What a happy time in the planning this was going to be.

"Oh, Sugar, here. Don't cry," I said and held her.

I thought it through and gave some suggestions. "Beth, can you let your mother have a wedding—and can we get married?"

The idea appealed to her, though she was voiceless.

I went on. "Beth, our wedding day is approaching and I have finals. Just encourage your mother to make decisions and get it done. Is that okay?"

"Yes, she just makes me mad."

I used the gift of restraint and changed the subject to lighten the load a few tons.

On the Neuro final, Mike had bonus questions with required narrative answers. The one I chose sounded easy. He asked us to describe every pathway used when a woman asks a man for a quarter and he reaches into his pocket and gives it to her. I envisioned the butcher paper on the wall at home and answered the question accurately. It took six pages. My confidence was high. Because I had set the curve on the final exam, some classmates wanted to stone me. I felt pretty brassy for an old route man.

We would marry the day after Christmas and it would be an elegant affair, just as Beth's mother intended. Julie Case spent too much money and I was surprised Harry didn't croak. She upset most everyone involved in the wedding plan that she created. Beth and I went along for the ride with our eyes wide open and mouths shut.

For over two hours, Beth and her mother visited with Mona and my mom at their bakery about the catering details. Mrs. Case said she was going to go somewhere else and did. Beth was stunned and Mona wanted to punch her. My mom wanted to make the groom's cake, but Julie Case believed in one cake. In her way of thinking, it wasn't a bride and groom, but a union, so she flagged the groom's cake.

Mom cried over Mrs. Case's decision. She was defiant. "I will make the groom's cake if I have to leave it on the steps of the church."

At the rate things were going, I hoped there wouldn't be a fistfight at the ceremony. Replacing our choice from the Book of Ruth, Beth's mom chose other invitations. Her mother didn't know those verses were sentimental. Beth wrote the words in one of her letters and I kept it forever in my Bible. The wedding photographer chose to quit several times. He pulled Beth aside at the wedding and confided in her that he had planned to not show up, but rethought it and couldn't no-show because he felt sorry for her.

As planned, Beth and I married in the church with a honeymoon in Cancun. We were exhausted from the preparations and the Christmas holiday, but we managed to recite our personalized vows. Tubby was my best man. He joined Ron and Michael P, the two other henchmen I chose to escort the ladies in

Hodge Wood

the ceremony. The three looked dapper in their formal tuxedos that Mrs. Case had chosen. My anxieties decreased as all three followed my orders and made it on time and close to sober.

The wedding, with Beth as the centerpiece, turned out beautiful. I was amazed at what the Cases' hard-earned money could buy. The cake and punch reception went okay, except for a couple of my friends and their uninvited guests who showed up on drugs and alcohol. At the end of the reception, Beth shot her garter over her shoulder in traditional fashion. My time-tested friend, Alan, fought for the garter with a rebel yell and pulled it over his bald head with several vicious dog barks. I wasn't sure what kind of stimulants and depressants he had taken. Beth and I ran to change clothes and to make our getaway.

Tubby stuck his head in the dressing room. "Get out of here! Someone beat up your driver!"

Beth and I ran out of the church under the birdseed thrown in the air.

Dr. Dick Hill and his wife Gail planned to drive us to Dallas. We got in the car and they were mad as hornets. A heated argument got physical over painting their car with wedding graphics. Someone made quick work of Dr. Hill and finished off his ailing knee. We apologized, found a secluded spot and snuggled together in the back seat. Dick and Gail dropped us off at the airport hotel. We loved the night away before flying out to Mexico.

What goes around comes around. We heard a drunken brawl ruined Julie Case's wedding to Harry five children ago. I wished that it weren't true but couldn't help but see the irony between theirs and ours. Life is full of knee-slapping surprises.

Bathrooms in Paradise

Cancun was an uncrowded paradise in December of 1980. The turquoise blue water placed me in a trance. I stood upon the white sand and gazed across the ocean. Beth and I ate three squares a day consisting of the best fruit, ale and fixings. Our major responsibility was to remain affectionate. We maintained a submissive service.

On the second day at the beach, I lay down at the water's edge and let the waves roll me up and down like a log until I had difficulty getting up and walking. Beth and I left the beach for our room and noticed others watching me. The attention was obvious.

We shut our room door to get naked. I pulled my Speedo swim trunks down and a pound of sand flew out. Others thought I had packed my pants on the beach and that's why they looked. I rolled up all the sand that my trunks could hold and my butt bulged. The scenario was as comical as Beth's nude tan lines were exciting.

We drowned on tequila that night. I woke up with an ax in my head. We planned a simple tour bus ride to the Mayan ruins. That was about all I could handle. I was not in the mood to hear a brass band and sat on the bus, resting up to get ready for bed. Beth and I sat hung over in the front seat, getting nervous as the driver almost splattered several bicyclists along the narrow road through the jungle. The demon, "Mr. No Bowel and Bladder Control," decided to make me pay for my foolishness the night before.

Beth commented quietly, "Someone must be sick."

I was bleeding off gas like an oil refinery. "Sorry—it's me." Suddenly, all my sensors told me it was time to take an immediate bathroom break. "How much further?" I asked the driver. "I'm sick."

Hodge Wood

The driver and everyone turned green due to my fumigation. "Maybe five miles," he said. The driver couldn't pull over on the shrunken speedway.

Normally, Beth and I respect moderation when we drink. That wasn't the case the night before. The peyote god penciled me in on the "To Be Tortured List." My name had reached the top.

We pulled into the Tulum ruins and I stood in the bus door, looking for an outhouse like a kid for an ice cream truck. The bus was still rolling when I bailed out.

I asked the villagers, who couldn't speak English, "Where are the bathrooms?"

Desperate and fearful, I scanned the village ruins to a place that appeared to be a restroom. I got there as fast as I could stumble. I might deliver the tourist package in my bowel on any step. A one-legged man at the bathroom door requested pesos with a handful of wipes extended my way. He stopped me and my bomb door began to open. Beth had our money and she continued on in the bus. Since I knew I could not whip a one legged man in the Mayan ruins over the cost of toilet paper, I spoke in tongues and emphasized the urgency I faced. My system didn't wait. I waddled past the one legged man into the bathroom and had a mess all the way down my legs after overflowing my swim trunks. I was hung over, mad, embarrassed beyond recovery—and coated in crap in a remote region of a foreign land.

I entered the toilet stall to find it full of brown dung water. Even more pleasing was the reality that no running water existed. I was having a memorable time in an exotic location on my honeymoon.

My illness had affected every tourist on the bus, so they directed Beth to find me before going sightseeing. Beth bought a large handful of toilet paper, but the one-legged man took pesos and she only had American dollars that first had to be exchanged. He didn't charge her to enter and assist me. If he had been selling guns I would have been history. Instead, I grabbed the wipes and ran her off. I let her know I saw the ocean about a quarter of a mile away and would go there alone. Screw the rules to not leave the group.

A few hundred pesos of toilet paper wouldn't repair the train wreck I was trying to fix. My hung-over, crap-covered ass became chapped as I looked at the porcelain seat in front of me. I had not felt a complete appreciation for the situation I faced until then. The toilets were wall mounted—not plumbed. I cried out, "Jesus Jones —you're shitting me!" I was in the fix of a lifetime.

I had no choice. I removed my soiled trunks and field cleaned my funky body with them. It was less effective than a sling shot in a tank battle. Another thought crossed my mind. I would have to return to the public square of Tulum. It was not a pretty picture, but thankfully, no one would have anything to do with me, which helped.

I avoided eye contact and marched into the village. I read the terrain and found seclusion at the ocean. Considering I might be a shark meal didn't slow me down. I swam into the salt water and removed my trunks to clean them. They became a washrag. I rubbed a few layers of skin off, sanitized my carcass and returned exhausted. I had all the fun I could take and waited in the shade to reload the bus.

Once on board, we had another stop in a small park named Xel Ha that was under development. We would swim there in a beautiful lagoon. Before we got there, I had to pee. I noticed pulling in that there weren't enough trees to hide and whiz. They hadn't finished any buildings so a flowing toilet might be hard to find. Beth and I planned a bathroom expedition like two GI's on a search and destroy mission. We spread out and stayed in touch. I barked commands. "You see about that building—it looks like a gift shop. I'll check that grassy hut—it's a bar." My last instruction came in full stride with Beth two paces behind me. I had no time to spare before springing a leak.

I apologized to God for drinking so much tequila and asked for mercy. My leg had multiple spasms while I was attempting not to lose bladder control. The Mexican heat beat me. I approached a concrete structure with a grassy top. Beth circled my way.

She said, "No bathrooms back there."

Two bathroom entries faced each other up ahead. I approached with a full load of water to pour out at any time. I stepped into the entry with my weak right leg and looked up for a sign. A piece of cardboard distracted my eyes—a small, torn piece hung on the wall at eye level that read, "No."

It happened suddenly. "Kabaam—Kaboom!" Somebody shot me twice and the sound rang in my head.

Nobody shot. I fell and hit my head twice. The cardboard sign caused me to look straight ahead, so I never saw the downward step of concrete and had no chance to negotiate my footing in the slimy overflow. I had rapidly slipped sideways, gained momentum on the lower level and the force spun me around backwards. The back of my head hit the concrete wall that held the "No" sign and the force of the blow must have dazed me. Halfway knocked out, I then slid further in the muck to crash on the masonry below like a big timber—colliding a second time on the back of my head.

My story differed from Beth's after the second blow to the head. I thought I tried to get up and reached for help from two Mexicans. Beth heard my skull bounce twice. She said the two Mexicans ran to pick me up as my dally-wagger stuck out of the bottom of my trunks and peed all over me. I don't remember whizzing, but never took a harder punch to my gourd. I lost my left sided vision for several minutes, an obvious trauma to my visual cortex.

Beth helped me locate the shade. She cried and wondered how to say neurosurgeon in Spanish. Once I could see again, my head was on fire. Although Beth discouraged me, I had to go float in the cool water to put out the Bunsen burner flame that lit in my globe. The multicolored tropical fish helped soothe my pain.

Chum Water

I floated and wondered, "Why me?"

My mind kept replaying the night before when Beth and I inhaled several tequila slammers. I swore off tequila and learned my lesson — the hard way as usual.

The Tulum ruins and Xel Ha Park would later have hotels and all the improvements. Everybody would swim the beautiful turquoise blue water in Tulum that was off limits when I cleaned up alone there. I am sure the crowds overflow and the tequila, too. I bet everyone has a ball, but I would never go back. The experience was a Tsunami in the currents of my life and the tidal wave closed the door.

The rest of our Cancun honeymoon was casual. We were lucky to be there before the big crowds noticed that Cancun was a breathtaking tropical destination. Beth and I spent pleasant and uneventful times. We smelled the sea and flowers over romantic meals and from gazebo views and tanned on the beach. We spoke of the future and of the past and made lots of love. Time stood still.

Hodge Wood

Six ~ Sea World

Patrol the Captured

St. Anthony Hospital is an old structure with respected services. I arrived the first day of my OT internship with the green-apple-two-step dictating bathroom visitation. They said not to drink the water in Mexico. I didn't but I did have the Exlax-ized ice. If not nervous enough with the start of my psych rotation, the drizzlies had me on high alert. I just made the walk from the parking garage to the john before leaving an emergency donation of my insides for the umpteenth time. After forty-eight hours of pit stops, I felt like the emcee on a toilet telethon. I continued to the locked inpatient psychiatric ward. I was concerned that I would not do well during my three-month stay. A short time passed before my prediction came true.

Once inside the locked ward, I tried to be positive but got over it fast. Two registered OT's named Jacquelyn and Roberta supervised me. They seemed depressed. Once it was obvious I was out of place and in the way, introductions began with support staff. Patsy and Wanda were kind. They were counting sharp tools like pencils and paper scissors before starting a treatment session. The place was a zoo. I grazed along to determine where to locate my carcass in the cage.

In her office, Jacquelyn began to orient me. "Be careful. Joe shot and killed his mother and may . . ."

Roberta interrupted, angry and close to tears. "I cannot put up with this group anymore . . . but anyway, Hodge—come join it."

We entered a room filled with patients at a table. Roberta gave me no names even though I was new. Most patients were depressed or schizophrenic. They were either withdrawn or angry. Roberta was quick to argue—I didn't cue in why the flak hit. The room heated up with disagreements and our planned group discussion went out of control. Withdrawn patients closed off. Those who were angry got more upset. The hostilities festered until Roberta claimed the therapy session was over and made an abrupt exit to the office. I followed like a fawn behind a doe.

Roberta wrote chart notes from the OT group that we had just left and directed me to review them. I read her sanitized version on each patient. I couldn't tie anything in to what had happened. All I saw was penned smoke and mirrors. Roberta hammered me with questions for which I had no answers—not one. I had to use a bobble-head nod. Roberta viewed her watch and declared it was time for the next therapeutic craft session. She said I would catch on and gestured me out to the OT work area to learn to patrol the captured.

I heard my voice say, "Please pass the colored pencils out." I was in charge.

Jacquelyn and Roberta were in their first year of OT practice. The rule was to wait until year two to become a fieldwork supervisor. They stretched it to have enough fieldwork sites for training numskulls like me. The three-month rotation was a nightmare that I had to pass through. Failure meant no chance to get registered and work.

Every day seemed the same. We reported on how medicine changed behavior. Light drooling during activity was acceptable. Being alert enough to take issue with anything was unacceptable. The OT sessions were Thorazine parties. I wished I had some. It was common for discharged patients to return. I never felt competent and got worse. I did as told. The cloning prepared me.

I learned to write tidy progress notes under the Gestapo style of supervision. When the therapy session time was over, it was over —even if a patient jumped from a window. As time elapsed, I learned to call the curtain. I read patient histories when they showed up, as taught in OT school. Sometimes others didn't to save time and that was a glaring error. I passed the rotation, didn't understand enough to help anyone and proved it was impossible for me to work in a psychiatric service. The ward door locked behind me for the last time. I looked forward to going to Baptist Medical Center for my final internship in physical disability.

Where I Came From

Mona scheduled mother to work as many hours as she would take at the bakery. Mom would then go home and take care of dad. He had lost his mental faculties long ago. The Lucky Strikes that dad inhaled most of his life had done their damage and left him with emphysema, requiring oxygen. Dad was a full-time, round-the-clock job for mom. She had lost far too much weight, but refused to go to the doctor or change her schedule. Home care for dad was not affordable. Mom needed to earn all she could from her minimum wage. She always wore a smile and I guessed she had one stretched across her face while chopping tobacco and smoking a cigarette at the tender age of nine in North Carolina too.

A visit with mom as dad lay on the couch was difficult in the small frame house I grew up in. Mom and I sat at the table trying to converse. Dad couldn't hear without the TV blaring and he was unable to follow a story anyway. Nevertheless, he wanted it on.

"How is Beth, Sweetie?" Mom asked.

"Just fine, now at Presbyterian. Has a good job seeing people with head injuries," I said as she asked questions.

While sitting at the old black and white dining room table, we talked about my 1968 Plymouth GTX that mother drove. When I was in high school, I worked seven days a week to save the dough to get that muscle car. I left it with her when I went into the service because she didn't have any transportation. Mom kept the GTX in hopes I would want it back. With a 375 horsepower engine and no power steering, the machine was a basic drag racer.

"Mom, Bill next door said when you back out of the drive and pull forward, you lay rubber over the curb trying to get turned. Shouldn't you sell it?"

"No way, honey," she said smiling as she lit up a Winston. "I have fun going to work in it." She went on. "Kids pull up to me and I rev it up and look at them and they laugh. A cop pulled me over and told me to be careful. Don't you want it back?"

Before I could say no, dad interrupted.

"Eva, get this pillow out from under my legs. I can't breathe. Get out of here with that cigarette."

Mom extinguished her smoke with several other partial burns and ran to relocate the pillow. "There, Buford, is that better?"

"I wish I could breathe. Let Tiger out!" She hustled the poodle dog out the back door. On her way back through the kitchen dad said, "Eva, I can't breathe. Can you put a pillow under my legs?"

Dad gasped for air that his lungs could not process. He was suffocating slowly. Disease had shrunk his brain, forever removing the bright sense of humor he once possessed. Mom worked to replace the pillow in the exact position it had been in when she removed it. Dad kept her moving. I had to go.

"He is right, Momma, you should try to not smoke in here," I suggested and hugged her goodbye. "Good-bye, dad."

I was at the front door when he spoke. "You going somewhere? You just got home!"

"Dad, I don't live here anymore."

I stepped onto the porch and he gave mom a direction. "Eva, let Tiger out."

The dog was out. I knew the process went on day and night. There was nothing that could be done.

Chum Water

After driving up the block, I turned off the car at my childhood buddy Sid's old two-bedroom house. What happened there was not pretty. Late one night as young teenagers, Sid and I found his mother with her eyes beaten shut. She was drunk as usual. Rollie, his step dad, had worked her over again. Sid pushed his mom aside and motioned me in without words. Down the hall, I noted an empty fifth on the bedside table next to Rollie. He had passed out. Sid stared in silence from the hallway. I knew that a small wooden baseball bat lay in his bedroom a few feet away and figured Sid would get it to pound Rollie again. Sid tucked the covers in around Rollie so he would not be able to escape. Rollie snoozed. This time Sid used fists. He began to tenderize Rollie with multiple sharp blows.

Rollie yelled, "No, Sid, no!" He tried to get out, his head bouncing like it was on a trampoline, begging Sid for mercy. There wasn't any. Sid hammered away until I pulled him off.

Sid warned a battered Rollie. "Don't do it again!"

It happened all the time. Sid returned with me to his room and we sat down to read comic books.

That was a long time ago. Rollie and his mom no longer lived there. I smiled before I drove off because Sid became a Grand State Wrestling Champion and ran his own successful agency in our hometown. I hoped he was fine. We had lost contact.

I pulled two doors west, entered the boulevard and made a right into Tom and Ruth's house. I imagined Tom smiling at me from his recliner, saying, "Hi, Peckerhead." I missed him.

Ruth was fine and pleased to see me. She started driving after Tom died and carried on independently, against all bets she would not do well.

"Could I fix you something to eat?" Ruth asked.

"No thanks, Ruth." I continued. "I went by to see mom and dad and had a minute. Do you need anything?"

"No, just more sweet company from you and Beth is all. How is she?"

We made small talk for a few minutes before I had to go home. I explained that I started my clinical rotation Monday and took my occupational therapy registration exam in three months. When I spoke to Ruth about the technicalities of my pursuits, she understood little, but I could sense how happy Ruth was, like mom, because I had found my way.

Where I Was Going

Baptist Medical Center is a huge facility made of more brick and mortar than you could pile in twenty years. A strict German named Karen was the Chief OTR and my supervisor. Her reputation made me know I had to hustle to pass. Karen handed as much to her students as they wanted. Her grade measured against the ability to assume responsibility so I planned to be fast and learn how to carry a full patient load.

Karen could scare people. A new occupational therapist had employment opportunities with sign-on bonuses. Graduates attended recruitment fairs and employers pitched their settings because demand exceeded supply. Karen seemed to care less. I didn't mind. She didn't scare me. Baptist was a first-class facility and someday I would love to work there.

We started like a bolt of lightning. Karen spoke fast and her German accent made it hard to follow her. She defined her expectations, showed me the tools in the clinic and questioned me about evaluations that we hadn't covered in class. I listened. My first rotation kept me from bobbing my head when I became intimidated. I shot from the hip. My plan was simple — gobble up work to keep Karen happy. Students cost no money, just time. I left the first day anxious to get back.

It felt natural to be with my first patient. I said hello and Joe smiled. He had a word retrieval problem. A stroke in the left side of his brain weakened the right side of his body so he wasn't safe on his feet. His wife told me that Joe was a WW II veteran and that they owned a motor home. I evaluated and placed entries in the forms.

Joe asked, "You walk happy?"

I thought for a minute and knew he retrieved the wrong word. He had watched me walk and noted my impairment. I grinned. "Yeah, I walk funny." I sensed it was okay to joke with Joe about the serious side of life. "Pretty soon you will walk funny, too."

Joe had twenty pounds of right-hand grip with minor muscle tone problems. He had measurable pinch in each fingertip. Those were good signs. We could normalize his extremity tone, maintain range and gain control. Sensory testing was normal, as were his visual perceptual skills. The evaluation turned out to be not much more than that. Joe's stated goal was to walk. It was the most common patient comment I would hear in my life.

I described how we would work on the mat, do standing retrievals and walk later. I planned to use resistive patterns in the absence of high tone and progress to higher-level coordination skills. They understood.

Joe's wife asked, "How will he do?"

I said, "He has good rehab potential."

That was all a greenhorn student should say. Following strokes, no one can be sure. I thought Joe would heal spontaneously and felt fortunate that Joe was such an easy first catch. I knew patients would not all be so easy. I progressed to carry eight or more at once. Karen said that was more than previous students had done.

Karen hired another OT named Tommy from out of state. He was a pleasing therapist and Christian—the perfect role model for me. I gained skills and Tommy said I would do well as a therapist. He suggested I not overdo. I gave a full effort and that freed Karen up for other duties.

Rodney came into the OT Department on a gurney from the Burn Unit where he had been for months. He was positive for a man in his twenties dealing with a severe blow. An oil rig exploded and he nearly burned up. Worse, Rodney had run out of skin graft donor sites while upstairs. Rodney's hands, feet and ears melted down and his disfiguring injury added to the damage to his lungs and eyes.

"It was a miracle he lived," someone said.

I thought back to the patient, Joe, at the hospital in Memphis. His head was zilched off by electrocution. People said Joe's living was a miracle. I never thought so. The personal nature of critical injury allows no chance to sugarcoat the truth.

At first, Rodney was happy to be out of the burn unit—but it was short-lived. While we continued to stretch his painful body that had survived hell, Tommy and I knew that we were limited. We gave range, position assistance and family education. Rodney had a young wife who would learn fast. I oriented him to available chin-driven controls. There wasn't much else we could do.

At discharge, we set up a nursing home placement for Rodney. When they took him away, Tommy and I laughed with Rodney like we did when all patients left. These final visits were sad underneath the camaraderie. It came with the territory.

Becky was a slender woman who drove a red Corvette. She had had a hip replaced and came to the clinic to learn how to transfer and dress with respect for hip precautions. Her spectacular looks took me—and I fought to hide it. After surgery, she wasn't supposed to cross her legs or bend her replaced hip beyond ninety degrees. With relative professional composure, we practiced transfers and dressing with adaptive aides. Experience was yet to be on my side. Becky was never concerned, but being fresh out of school caused me difficulty. Helping in her personal space made me a nervous wreck.

One day in the private room, Becky looked at me with a smile and asked sincere questions. "How about positions for sex—what positions do you recommend or think I should avoid?"

A twenty-amp male fuse blew in my system when I heard her words. She seemed to get a kick out of how hard I tried to keep my response on the appropriate level. A couple of ideas came out in stammered and stuttered phrases. My lips flopped off my nose and chin. I needed a wench to get my tongue back in my mouth. For some reason, I continued speaking. "The intensity of sexual activity needs consideration—the jarring forces might cause harm." No resource had taught me that and freelancing wasn't a good practice. Bailing out, I suggested she call her surgeon about the matter. Her questions were as genuine as my answers.

She continued to smile and thanked me.

I felt like asking if I could go now, but closed the session with a learned line. "Becky, the treatment session time is up."

I saw many stroke patients. They experienced light to severe damage. Stroke rehab is a specialty for the occupational therapist and my work in college paid off. I learned to use Karen's tools. The brain is sacred. Damage it and the patient may lose control of limbs, lose speech and other abilities. There are subtle losses at times. I could identify and treat the bunch.

One banker couldn't sequence. He was unable to fold a piece of paper, place it in an envelope and seal it—even though he knew what he intended to do. He couldn't put on his shirt or pants or fill out a check. A carpenter tried to brush his teeth with his comb. When asked to point to a hammer in the visual battery, he chose a lampshade. Another with a perceptual deficit went home and tried to drive his car in the wheat field, burying it high center. We predicted he would do it. A housewife was impulsive after her stroke. She could not sit up alone, but tried to get up without understanding the risk. I watched so she wouldn't catch her arm in the wheel of her chair. We had a long way to go before she might cook in the OT kitchen. We provided repetitive physical positioning and verbal correction to the point it seemed redundant. With tough back-to-back stroke patients, I sweated for hours and went home exhausted. Amputations, head injuries, multiple traumas, heart surgeries and knee replacements came through. We treated all over the hospital.

Looking forward to my week upstairs in the burn unit, I felt confident by the last month. It was more than just a learning experience down the stretch. It didn't pay, but I had a real job.

Galaxy

Beth and I talked about a new boat. We had repainted Old Blue and the whopping one hundred and three dollar house payment was our one monthly bill. Beth made good money. I would double it after June graduation. All winter, we courted the idea of getting a better boat and would use it most evenings. I sold the Wonderglas for what I had paid for it. We wanted more.

Beth and I came home with a small rig—a sixteen-foot silver metal flake Galaxy with an eighty-five horsepower Johnson. We installed a tall tow pylon. The higher angle of pull might make the difference for me to get up on skis. Beth and I bounced around in the new boat parked in our driveway. We sat under the stars, toasted with a fresh bottle of champagne and added the cork to the collection.

I called mom with the news and agreed to take her fishing. Her cough seemed worse, but she denied it. I couldn't hide my excitement about everything going on. I said, "Mom, watch the mail. Your invitation is coming to go to the graduation ceremony for the 'Senior Class of Occupational Therapy at the Health Sciences Center.'"

Mom was so pleased her tears spilled out as she coughed away. She said, "I can't wait! I am so proud of you."

Things were going my way.

Game to Try

I entered the ICU to see a new patient, pulled his chart at the nursing station and jotted history notes on an index card. I chatted with the nurse.

I read about my new twenty-one year old patient, Bobby Jack Carter. He had severed his aorta and broken both legs. I wondered why he didn't bleed to death on the highway after this main artery from his heart was cut. They repaired the artery and spared his life, but his friend died. The men were doing seventy in a pickup. In the dark, a flatbed from a rig site pulled onto the two-lane highway. They never even hit the brake and crashed underneath. While repairing Bobby Jack's aorta, a surgical error cut the supply of blood to his spinal cord. It first went unnoticed, so Bobby Jack was a paraplegic.

I walked into his room to begin evaluation. Bobby Jack was in critical condition. I placed my hand on his shoulder and caught eyes to note equivalent dilation.

"Hello, Bobby Jack. How are you doing?"

"Okay, I guess," Bobby Jack said with a slow Okie drawl.

"I am Hodge Wood from the Occupational Therapy Department and I would like to initiate your treatment with an evaluation."

In a simple but alert fashion, he said, "Okay."

He had company—a big man with one eye. I smiled at them as I gestured. "Bobby Jack, is this your bodyguard? He won't hurt me will he?"

A smile flashed on their faces. "This is my dad."

I shook Mr. Carter's bear-sized, rough hand. I could have struck a match on it. "Nice to meet you, Mr. Carter. I hope to help you guys and will try to answer questions. Bobby Jack has been through the mill. I need to determine where to begin."

"Thank you, it's appreciated," Mr. Carter said with a slower drawl than his son's.

Bobby Jack had deep wounds stapled or stitched up. His entire body was black and blue. Any movement I elicited caused him to wince. I addressed working with pain. "Bobby Jack, please work within acceptable pain levels. Stop me before it is too much. We are going to have to spend weeks together and I don't want to wear out my welcome."

According to his chart, Bobby Jack had no fractures above his legs. I used my tools to measure decreased range in his upper body and arms. These losses were due to pain or chest wall adhesion. We could hope for gains and I wanted to remeasure often. I would have to fish for encouraging things to show him. As busted up as he was, I needed to be sure nothing got worse because I had suspected that there might be some uncharted injuries. Most crushed up people receive other injuries that aren't initially found. I raised his bed sheet to see where the surgeons had cracked open his chest. Then I moved his catheter bag and viewed both thighs. Giant staples held bright red incisions closed from the top of his legs to his kneecaps. Bobby Jack moaned as I took measures of his legs. His contractures concerned me. Neither leg had active movement, but I could bend them a little.

I told Bobby Jack that we would double up with the physical therapist and stretch his legs each day. I leveled with him. "It will be painful."

He had the heart of a lion, tried to be pleasant and his manners were simple. "I just wanna get well. What can you do first?"

I explained we would range his arms, shoulders and chest. Once he could tolerate side-sitting in bed, it would give me the best position to start trying to bend his legs. He nodded and smiled. He still might not live and I knew it would take months to recover. Bobby Jack was game to try.

Bone Deep

The spring evening was perfect except there was no breeze. The house felt fresh. The May air created a quiet and relaxed effect. I rubbed Walter's long ears and he responded with approving basset hound moans. The phone rang and Beth answered. She was startled. It broke the comfort.

Beth spoke. "It was your dad. He said your mom was bleeding and needed an ambulance—to come quick. He hung up."

I floored it with the flashers on to their place about seven miles away. I asked Beth for clarification. "Did he say what happened? Maybe cut herself?"

"No, he said nothing else."

I tried to be rational as dad's mind was gone. "Daddy isn't reliable. I bet it's nothing serious." I turned off the flashers for a hundred yards, slowed down, but sped back up and clicked them on again.

I cruised to a stop on the curb and I looked across the yard to see dad through the window. He walked across the living room floor in the same slow fashion. Every light in the house was on. All seemed well, so I calmed down. I stepped towards the house and looked up at the stars illuminating on a moonless, motionless, soundless night. At the base of the porch in the pitch darkness, I tripped and fell face to face with my mother in a pool of blood. She made a gurgling noise. Horrified, I screamed, "Beth, call 911!"

Mom's eyes were ballooned open and frozen in place. She had lung tissue and false teeth hanging out of the corner of her open mouth and blood coagulated all over her and down the walkway. She looked gory lying there in her house robe.

I said, "Come on Momma! Don't go!"

I drug the lung tissue and false teeth out of her mouth to try to clear an airway and began CPR. She had no breath or pulse.

Hodge Wood

Initiating mouth to mouth, I could taste her blood and heard the gurgling again. Beth returned to assist me with CPR until the ambulance crew took over. The neighbors and my sister gathered.

The ambulance crew worked. I sat short of breath on the same porch steps I played on as a boy. It was too vivid. My mind went hazy.

I sat on towels and rode to the hospital covered in blood. Mom was dead on arrival.

Later they said she had coughed up her lung and esophagus due to the undiagnosed cancer. She saw a doctor but he never scoped her. He treated her for a cold. We determined mom tried to run next door for help, but never made it before coughing up her tissues.

I felt guilty. Yesterday, mom agreed with me to check into a nursing home for dad. She visited a day center after leaving the bakery. We talked afterwards. Mom felt bad about placing dad. I invited her to fish, which was all she liked to do, but I hadn't taken her in a long time. Her final words rang in my ears.

She said, "Oh, Honey, I will go as soon as I get over this cough."

I would never get to take her fishing again.

The next morning, I called Karen. It was difficult to describe the tragedy. I let her know I needed time to bury mom and find a nursing home for dad.

Karen didn't seem compassionate. "Hodge, you are allowed to miss three days, according to guidelines. I am sorry. You haven't missed any time since you started and that is good. I expect you back after three days."

Her being short flattened me.

She shifted to business with a demanding tone. "Can you tell me about your patients so I can secure coverage?"

Astonished by her lack of consideration, I managed to share what to do with my patients. Karen treated me as if I had called in for a vacation. I didn't want to see her again, but mustered the courage not to say it. Karen said if I didn't make it back in time, I'd have to repeat my rotation somewhere else. My mother's death was inconvenient for her. I got angry and wondered if Karen should be in health care. She delivered compassion with a sledgehammer. I proposed the idea of returning in four days to the burn unit and said good-bye. I disliked being Karen's boy.

Disgust for the health care system grew in the midst of my grief. I thought over situations faced since I broke my neck. Those in charge may not be decent people. In fact, behind the scenes, there are many abusive sharks disguised in lab coats. I had an inside look. I couldn't relax anymore. What had I gotten into? My street smarts became useful again. Raped of my perception that people in health care were all caring souls with whale-sized hearts, I put up the defenses others used. Falling to their superficial level made things easier. There were "Hammerheads" in this line of work and I had to be careful. I sized everyone up.

We buried mom. I returned to work, said little about the last three days, took it on the chin and never blinked. Good impressions returned on the respected burn unit as we served patients in a gutsy way. I felt like Rocky—beaten up and still punching to go the distance. I saw the true color of the health care system during the infancy of my occupational therapy practice. It took away much of my confidence that I had a calling.

Beverly took dad to her house until we could find a placement home. She described how hard he was to manage. Dad called out for mom around the clock. My brother-in-law almost put him out of his misery for keeping them up all night. We could not imagine how mom had managed.

We found a nursing home that we liked but there was a waiting list. Until there was an opening, we had to put him in another one. Dad told me not to leave him in a rest home the first day. They had him tied in a chair on my second visit. He drooled away, zoned out on medication. Dad was done for life.

I took Dad out to eat but the change was disorienting. He sorted his silverware and didn't recognize Beth. Dad asked adamantly. "Where's Eva?"

"Dad, she's dead."

"That's right," he quipped, said no more and went back to sorting.

Bev and I transferred dad to the other rest home, but it was too late for him to recognize the improvement. He wouldn't last a year after mom died.

We cleaned out our home we grew up in on Rose Drive. I found a treasure in every dresser drawer. The flea market people took it all for dimes on dollars in a front yard sale. Anxiety surfaced as tragedy gut punched me. There was no time to recover. After mom bled to death, I no longer dreamed. Reoccurring nightmares relating to my mother's death at 756 Rose filled my nights. The 756 nightmares would always return. I hurt bone deep.

Back At the Ranch

I returned to the OT Department to finish my internship and Tommy gave me a warm hug. He said, "I've been praying for you."

That meant a lot and I asked that he keep it up. Karen had asked him to get me rolling while she managed things elsewhere. His speedy patient update took little time. I hit the floor running.

The charge nurse upstairs asked, "Where have you been?"

I suspected Karen said nothing about mom's death since I was just a student passing through. I didn't want attention and kept my eyes on the chart.

"Death in the family," I said, as if a long lost relative had passed from old age.

The nurse nodded. Bobby Jack moved to the floor from ICU and she had news. "Did you hear about Bobby Jack's sister? She's in 609 — broke her back in a car wreck."

"Jesus!" I gasped. The sea of agony and affliction continued to fill up. Bobby Jack's dad was on the hospital unit with two children paralyzed at either end of the hall.

"I will go see Bobby Jack."

We shook hands. "Great to see you, Bobby Jack. How are you doing?" I could imagine.

He said, "I'm okay. Sorry to hear about your mother. Are you okay?"

Tommy had told him. "I will make it, thanks. Bobby Jack, it looks like a gray cloud hangs overhead for your family. I heard about your sister. How is she and your dad?"

"Pretty hard on dad," is all he replied.

Therapy revealed he could do more and Bobby Jack was pleased. His balance improved to the point he could sit, without support, on the bedside. However, his leg paralysis showed no gains and I still couldn't bend his knees much. Complications and multiple traumas slowed him down and there was great concern not to bust open his healing aorta. We kept going.

We prolonged stretch to his knees. I laced my weaker arm under one leg and on top of the other to create a fulcrum. I applied maximum pressure with my strong arm to stretch him and repeated repetitions. He took the pain and focused to help move.

I sweat with the labor and readjusted my body to get up close in order to get a tight grip. I put my face inside his knees, right below his bottom. I said, "OK, Bobby Jack, last one — give it all you've got." He moaned with pain. As we harmonized our efforts, Bobby Jack released a large, trapped air pocket of gas in my face that went, "TTTTHHHBBB." I came up fast. We looked at one another and laughed until our sides hurt. Funny things happen on the ranch.

I treated Bobby Jack twice a day until I left Baptist Hospital. A couple of months later, he asked to continue rehab with me in another setting. It would be my pleasure to see him again and guide his path back into society.

Walter's Night Out

Since mother's death, Beth couldn't open closets and she was frightened of the dark. Time would heal, but our schedules were set at a rapid pace. I finished at Baptist Hospital in good shape, prepared to find a job and continued working out at the health spa.

Beth and I found comfort on the lake as summer arrived. She became an excellent slalom skier. Our Galaxy delivered plenty of power and I got closer to getting up on skis. We recharged our batteries and loved to anchor under the stars. One Saturday, we had a small bottle of Crown Royal to mix with Coke. We planned to melt into the boat and stay all night. After ten, I spread out the seats to make beds and broke the lid on the spirits.

With no intentions of leaving, we halved the bottle of Crown in our two plastic cups. We took a sip every now and then and left the cups below on the deck. We looked up at the stars and heard the waves lap against the hull. The lapping sound of the water against the boat relaxed us. In a vegetative state around midnight, we discovered that the lapping had stopped. Walter was the lapper, not the waves. Our Bassett hound drained every bit of whiskey and coke that we had left. He drank most of both highballs.

Walter bellowed out a drunken howl and threw slobber everywhere. He was so smashed he couldn't stay on his feet. Bassets and drunks slobber. Walter was both. He tried to jump up on us and we pushed him away. Beth and I doubled over with laughter, looking at such a pathetic sight. Walter stored up the slobber, shook his head and flung loogies. He seemed mad about his inebriated condition. He broke the silence of the night with quick, sharp howls. "Yaalp—Yaalp—Yaalp," echoed across the lake. Then he ran into the boat seats and fell over on his back.

Walter was such a lush that we had to isolate him in the front of the boat by placing the ice chest in his way below the center windshield so he couldn't join us. He was plastered and entertaining. Finally he gave it up, passed out in true alcoholic fashion and snored the night away.

Basset eyes are sad enough, but they were worse the next morning. He moaned with hangover agony. He tried to find a position of comfort to lie in, but there just wasn't one.

Beth asked, "What can you do?"

I fed Walter Tylenol, since the whiskey didn't kill him.

Male Marlin

I felt strong and listened to the boat engine rumble. Beth idled around before dark and fed the water ski rope handle to me in the lake. She checked a critical need. "You've gotten close. Do you have on a good pair of gloves?"

"New pair," I said.

It was my millionth attempt. I tried to come up so many times that the skin on my palm callused over and then raked off. I wore a bandage. When I failed to ski, I hung on and body surfed on my stomach—but there was no future in it. I had wanted to water ski for four years, despite my paralysis.

I used imagery to prepare to get up on skis. The routine had been ingrained. I favored my right leg by extending it further than I cared to place it. There was an exact position that my right ski had to be in to transition up. I had felt it on numerous attempts. I reviewed how to bunch the glove and cheat my right grip around the handle. My left hand took the initial surge on full throttle before adding pull in my right hand. If my grip held, I transferred more weight on my left leg and kept my right leg from running behind or skating away. I knew how but hadn't succeeded.

"I can do it," I said to myself, as always.

My mind drifted. I became the strongest inner tube rider on the lake—maybe in anticipation that I might not get up again on skis. However, I shut out inner tube thoughts to latch back on to the technical details of getting up on skis. Beth gained alignment to tow me. I scanned the glassy lake surface. My adrenaline rushed as I looked up the rope and said to idle out.

I yelled, "Hit it!"

As the Galaxy sped away, my right leg slipped into place and I added right grip. My heart pumped like a piston and I looked above the water and righted myself. The engine didn't miss a beat and I straightened my back. I was skiing! I relaxed with my right foot forward of the left. I laughed out loud and watched Beth do the same. I cut across the boat wake and carved a path. My right leg required adjustment on every inch of turbulent water that sped under me. I skied and felt refreshed with the pleasure of recreation that I had missed for so long. This fish was home on the water—jumping above the surface and flipping his tail. My gills opened and closed at full volume to absorb the air and feed my body. I was a male marlin, beautiful and strong in spirit. I cut back across the wake and let myself go. I never gave up my vision of being able to ski again. For an instant, I soaked in gratification. Then my right knee bent backwards due to residual paralysis and it drove the tip of my ski underwater. I did a face plant. There was no harm except my reddened face from smacking the lake. I cheered and Beth returned to get me. I saw her joy because I had fulfilled my dream.

I struggled with fatigue to get back into the boat and then squeezed Beth in mutual delight. We reconquered my favorite diversion. I improved into fall and began to attempt to slalom on the Jobe ski. I was so thankful that Beth had never given up on me.

My high school reunion fell in the middle of the occupational therapy registration examination. I had to pass the test to practice and get paid. The exam lasted all Saturday morning and it was my biggest academic challenge. My high school class produced community leaders and prison convicts. I wanted to see as many lawmen and outlaws as I could at the reunion. Both events were important to me. I penciled in to attend them at the same time.

The reunion weekend had a variety of events, but the cultural affair that most interested me was the keg party. We tapped the keg in the park I grew up in, located across the street from Ruth's house. We showed up Friday for all the beer we could drink—and to swap old stories. It took all night. I never went to bed.

I arrived on schedule at eight the next morning at the College of Health to begin the intensive examination. I felt less than bright and shiny. Coffee provided a wake up—and I could pee at will to purge it. All of my OT classmates were scared to death before we started. Strangers, who had failed the exam on earlier dates, came and they looked like death row inmates. After the test was over in the afternoon, the heat got to me. I went home to rest rather than return for the reunion festivities. More often than before in life, common sense prevailed. I chalked it up to having a bright future. When the results came in, I had passed. I only needed a job.

Follow the Red Dots

I wanted to work at the new O'Donoghue Rehabilitation Institute. Parking was convenient and that was unusual for the Medical Center. I had accepted the use of a handicapped parking card and they had a dozen freshly painted spots out front. The new center was to grow and the chance to join a large staff excited me. I had seen the huge OT/PT gym on the main floor and it was state-of-the-art. I scheduled an interview with great anticipation.

Emke Druding was the Chief of Occupational Therapy who could offer a job. I waited for her not knowing what to expect. Her secretary, who had a British accent that made her sound like a Monte Python character, spoke to the patients arriving for therapy. Six days seemed to pass before the invitation came to enter the private office behind the waiting room. I stepped that way.

I greeted Emke. She shook my hand with a poker face and slammed the door shut behind me.

She said authoritatively, "Sit down."

My butt hit the chair.

She got a phone call and I asked, "Should I step out?"

Emke said, "Sit down!"

She seemed a little short with my offer for privacy. I stayed put.

Emke was sharp and spoke with power on the phone. She was a decision maker and in control, judging from her call. I looked at things in the room while she talked. Her office had class and personality. Her wall held many framed shingles, including her OT Registration with another last name. I gazed at a big picture of her on her knees in a bikini in the front of a canoe, stretched out like a georgous ship sculpture from the eighteen hundreds. Emke had knockout good looks and a big-breasted body. The snapshot was quite daring for an office setting. Recognizing how tall and beautiful she was in person made me nervous. My emotions were already mixed up. I liked her attractive appearance, but was scared of her dominant nature. All she had said to me was to sit down twice. It took a few seconds to get a grip and calm down. I checked her closer. Emke wore a white business dress that accentuated her killer looks. I had never seen another OT dress that well—more like an attorney than a therapist. While I was still deep in thought over her looks, she slammed the phone down to end her call.

"Oh, yes, where were we?" she asked.

Based on her question, I felt compelled to flash a smile and remain factual. I reminded her that she had scheduled me for an interview and related I was a new grad and thankful for her time.

Emke left me hanging. I caught a brief glimmer of acceptance in her attractive eyes and she pointed out the window that overlooked the large therapy gym. "Do you think you could work out there?" she asked. Emke implied it would be no small chore.

"Yes, I would be delighted to try. I rolled around in a smaller gym as a patient and I think that might have been harder than working out there."

She left me hanging again. Emke continued looking across the treatment floor long after my answer floated her way and then turned to speak in a matter-of-fact fashion. She briefed me on the physical lay out, the growth intent, expectations, salary and benefits. I thought she might say, sign here quick—I have work to do, but that didn't happen. We shared answers to questions and she seemed ho hum about me. The phone rang again. Emke answered it and said, "Sit down!"

I was already sitting.

While Emke was on the phone, I wondered what I was doing wrong because my answers were on key but she seemed unimpressed.

Emke hung up and walked past me saying, "Let's go. I will show you around."

We didn't catch eyes. I couldn't figure out why she was so flat. Emke had long beautiful legs. She remained about ten paces ahead of me no matter how fast I tried to go. As we walked to the main elevator, I realized the problem. On the back of her white dress was a trail of red bloodstains originating just below her bottom. The red stains dotted her dress in irregular circles and streaks all the way down the back of her legs. The red blotches terminated at her hem. Bless her heart—Emke was on her period.

She walked me through the entire center, maintaining the ten-pace advantage. I kept wondering if I should tell her about the bloodstains and worrying what might happen if I did. I decided to just follow the red dots. Emke shook my hand good-bye and said she would make decisions next week.

I mulled over the experience. I was a victim of queer circumstance if I missed the job.

When Emke invited me back, she was in far better spirits. We had a great meeting and she extended an offer. Of all places, my career would start on the Spinal Cord Injury Service! The job provided an attractive salary with exceptional state benefits. Had I ever come full circle.

I accepted, more thrilled than a skydiver. I hurried home to prepare dinner for the most beautiful woman in the world and kept the hire decision a surprise for later. I cooked and waited with champagne on ice to celebrate with Beth. She was my world.

My mind shot from the past to the present. It scattered. How did I make it?

God destined me. Mike Kuns saved my life. Bev and Ruth deserve medals. I wish Barb knew I had crawled out of the toilet. I will pray for her. Momma's spirit puts my face on. Never give up. Michael P's friendship makes my soul rumble like his Harley. What would I do without football? That colonel had a good idea. Skynyrd lives. A street survivor is a care provider. A jet will land on a jaguar.

Chum Water

Dinner was ready and the recliner had a tight grip on me. I had a deal again after four years of scratching and clawing my way back. The OT job would sure beat throwing glass-bottled pop off of a truck. Hard work, a lot of luck and the grace of God paid big dividends. I hoped to make a big splash in open water.

Hodge Skis Again!

Index

adaptations, 24, 39, 68
AFL-CIO, 25, 26
AIDS, 44, 66, 98
    Acquired Immune Deficiency Syndrome
anesthetized, 20, 52
    Not sensitive to pain or touch
ape hangers, 106
    Motorcycle handlebars that curve high above the machine
aphasic, 25
    Inability to express oneself properly through speech or loss of verbal comprehension
Appalachians, 128
Arkansas, 72, 73, 74, 77
    Bull Shoals, 72

Barbara, 2, 6, 18, 19, 22, 23, 35, 48, 49, 52, 63, 64, 65, 68, 69, 72, 73, 74, 75, 76, 77, 78, 79, 80, 81, 84, 85, 86, 87, 88, 89, 90, 91, 93, 122, 123, 168
bathroom, 1, 20, 42, 43, 45, 50, 64, 65, 79, 95, 111, 139, 140, 141, 142, 145, 168
Bible, xii, 27, 136, 137
bladder, 8, 31, 32, 38, 49, 50, 63, 70, 73, 95, 115, 139, 142
blood pressure, 25, 26, 38
bone, 17, 30, 65, 78, 99, 157, 160
Booker, 28, 29, 30, 31
bowels, 12, 13, 43, 44, 68
boxing, xi, xii, 3, 39, 77

Carter, Bobby Jack, 155, 156, 161, 162
catheter, 8, 12, 31, 32, 49, 56, 156
    Tube for evacuating fluids
catheterization, 31, 49
    Inserting a catheter
Chemical Dependency Unit, 20
chronology, 44
    Sequence of events

cigarettes, 10, 19, 37, 47, 69, 70, 79, 147, 148
    Lucky Strikes, 147
clonus, 61, 65, 75, 77
    Neurological muscle pathology marked by involuntary alternation of contraction and relaxation
Cock of the Walk Bar, 128, 129, 130, 134
College Date
    Barbara, 101, 102
control, 2 13, 41, 50, 51, 52, 53, 54, 61, 62, 63, 65, 73, 77, 83, 91, 92, 95, 96, 116, 121, 124, 133, 139, 142, 146, 151, 153, 166
courage, xii, 19, 69, 100, 159
cowboy up, 92
    Rodeo term, meaning to overcome serious hardship or injury and try again
Crown Royal, 162
    Premium blended Canadian "whisky"

dancing, 3, 51
depression, 86
    Mental state of mind identified by hopelessness and a lack of cheerfulness
Dicarlo, Steve, 21
Disco club, 1
Dodge, 5, 7
Donnell, Dodie, 58
dorsal, 21
Druding, Emke, 166
drugs, 8, 31, 32, 36, 95, 138

emphysema, 147
    Lung disease where cells rupture and lose elasticity resulting in inadequate oxygen exchange
endurance, 3, 39

Farr, Charles, 71
fascia, 98
    Membrane that covers, supports, and separates muscles and unites skin and tissue
Faulk, Steve, 81
Ferguson, Dr. Mike, 97, 133

football, 7, 10, 15, 35, 39, 43, 45, 52, 53, 54, 55, 56, 59, 81, 94, 103, 104, 108, 109, 110, 112, 116, 168
fusion, 24, 30, 35, 72, 75

genitalia, 99, 119
    Reproductive organs
God, 3, 6, 7, 8, 10, 28, 30, 35, 36, 47, 48, 50, 58, 59, 60, 62, 67, 71, 72, 73, 87, 91, 92, 103, 114, 117, 120, 123, 126, 130, 133, 136, 140, 142, 168, 169
Good Neighbors
    Shorty, 90, 91
    Tommy, 91
Graceland, 58
Grapes of Wrath, 27
gravity, 8, 20, 21, 23, 26, 37, 38, 39, 52, 75
Great Depression, 27, 78
    Time of extreme poverty in the 1930's
gurney, 10, 41, 46, 152

hallucination, 36
Harley Davidson, 34, 106
Hill, Dr. Dick, 138
Holiday Inn, 9

ICU, 9, 10, 11, 13, 15, 17, 18, 32, 37, 123, 155, 161
    Intensive Care Unit
Impala, 2
indwelling, 43, 49
    Internally placed, as in catheter
irrigated, 32
    Washed out with a fluid
IV, 10, 11, 12, 32, 34
    Intravenous

Jack Daniels Black, 90
    Tennessee whiskey
jaguar, 69, 70, 168
Jesus, 34, 48, 141, 161

kinesiology, 118
    Study of muscles and muscular movement

Kuns, Mike, 16, 19, 29, 40, 69, 168
    Guardian Angel

Lake Draper, 124
Lake Thunderbird, 107

medical students, 17
medication, 13, 20, 67, 160
Michael P, 33, 34, 52, 63, 64, 65, 81, 90, 106, 107, 108, 110, 119, 120, 122, 137, 168
mirrors, xi, 1, 2, 24, 28, 29, 39, 78, 88, 89, 113, 146
monitors, 10, 11
Morgan, Mark, 10, 20
Music Makers
    Bee Gees, 3
    Buffett, Jimmy, 5
    Eagles, 107, 115
    Fleetwood Mac, 89, 90
    Gaines, Steve, 5
    Heart, 65
    Lynyrd Skynyrd, 1, 5, 13, 14, 90, 91, 168
    Nelson, Willie, 64
    Nicks, Stevie, 90
    Orbison, Roy, 58
    Presley, Elvis, 54, 58
    Santana, 22, 110
    Seger, Bob, 23
    The Beatles, 110
    Van Zant, Ronnie, 5
    ZZ Top, 3, 22, 84, 88
myelogram, 12, 14
    Procedure to inspect the spinal cord for damage

National Geographic, 24
Nebraska, 55, 56, 58, 59
Neuro Ward, 18, 20
North Carolina, 55, 56, 57, 58, 59, 108, 112, 121, 125, 128, 147
    Blue Ridge Parkway, 128
    Chapel Hill, 112
Nurse Abuse, 25, 27, 28, 31

Nurse Assistant Slurspeech, 31, 49
nursing home, 16, 34, 152, 158, 160

O'Grady, Sean, xii
occupational therapist, xii, 23, 66, 134, 150, 153
Okie, 78, 155
    Someone from Oklahoma
Oklahoma, xii, 1, 5, 21, 22, 33, 55, 60, 62, 63, 65, 67, 70, 71, 77, 87, 104, 108, 111, 112, 126, 128
    Muskogee, 114
    Oklahoma City, 21, 22, 60, 62
    Tulsa, 22
orthopedics, 70
    Branch of medical science that primarily treats disorders of the skeleton, joints, muscles, and related soft tissues
OT, 23, 24, 47, 70, 71, 93, 94, 95, 96, 99, 102, 104, 107, 109, 112, 130, 145, 146, 147, 151, 152, 154, 160, 165, 166, 167, 169
    Occupational Therapy
    Evaluation and treatment directed at restoring function through purposeful activities after deficits are identified
OTR, 112, 150
    Registered Occupational Therapist
outpatient care, 16

paralysis, 7, 12, 13, 18, 20, 23, 27, 29, 34, 35, 41, 47, 57, 58, 69, 76, 77, 89, 90, 96, 101, 107, 113, 161, 164, 165
pathology, 97, 98, 100
    Study of the cause of disease and the conditions produced by disease
penis, 8, 31, 32, 99
Pepsi-Cola Bottling Company, 128
periscope, 24
physical therapist, 13, 17, 21, 38, 156
physiological, 22, 37, 39
    Normal, not diseased
posterior leaf, 52
    Non-hinged, standard issue foot orthosis to stop foot drop, made from high grade plastic

Reed, Dr. Kathlyn, 95, 96
Registered Dental Hygienist, 17

respiratory therapist, 11
Sanders, Ruth, 78, 79, 86, 87, 132, 133, 137, 149, 150, 165, 168
Sanderson, Professor Sharon, 93
Saturday Night Fever, 3
Schoenhals, Dr., 14, 15, 16, 30, 35, 72
screws, 16, 17, 18, 24, 26, 33, 36
Secanol, 20
sensory testing, 21, 151
Sims, Billy, 103, 109
Skaggs Albertson, 128
skin, 13, 16, 20, 27, 30, 38, 41, 46, 70, 80, 117, 120, 141, 152, 164
SKOAL BROTHER, 1, 8
Social Security, 26, 27
SOMI neck brace, 36
Sooner Magic, 104, 109
  Majestic circumstances that arise during Oklahoma football games
Sooner Schooner, 109
  Covered wagon pulled by two miniature ponies at Oklahoma football games
Sooners, 15, 55, 109
sores, 13, 16, 25, 27, 38, 41, 46, 60
spasms, 24, 73, 107
spasticity, 17, 42, 45, 49, 52, 61, 65, 66, 70, 75, 76, 95, 134
  Neurological muscle pathology marked by high tone causing stiff and awkward movements
spinal cord, 10, 15, 16, 21, 41, 74, 78, 91, 113, 134, 155, 168
sterile, 8
  Free from living microorganisms
steroids, 10
  Medication from an organic compound to reduce inflammation
Stryker Frame, 16, 18, 19, 23, 24, 25, 26, 28, 29, 30, 31, 32, 34, 35, 60
Swenson, Deb, 104
Switzer, Barry, 103, 104

therapists, xii, 11, 13, 17, 20, 21, 23, 66, 97, 134, 150, 151, 153, 156, 167
Thorazine, 146
  Medicine prescribed as a sedative to quiet severely excited psychiatric patients
Tommy, 151, 152, 160, 161
traction, 16, 18, 24, 25, 26, 35, 46
Twentieth Century Electric Light Company, 1, 3

Tylenol, 163
urethra, 32, 99
    Canal for discharging urine extending from the bladder to the outside
urine bag, 10, 42

VA, 10, 14, 21, 27, 42, 45, 57, 60, 61, 62, 63, 69, 72, 113, 114, 124
    Veterans Administration
Vandemeer, Steve, 33
Veterans Day Visiting Beauty Queens
    Miss Fort Gibson, 33
    Miss Indian America, 33
    Miss Rodeo Oklahoma, 33
Veterans Hospital, 9, 10, 21, 42, 69
Vietnam, 16, 54, 56, 57

Walter, 1, 29, 68, 90, 106, 115, 157, 162, 163
Ward 7 North, 18, 32, 41, 60, 70
Washington, Dave, 4, 7
water skiing. xi, 85, 88, 124, 164
Watts, JC, 103, 109
Wellington boots, 2, 8, 61, 67, 78
whiplash, 26
Wood, Beth Case, xii, 104, 105, 107, 108, 109, 110, 111, 112, 113, 114, 115,
    116, 117, 118, 119, 120, 121, 122, 123, 124, 125, 126, 127, 128, 130, 131,
    132, 133, 134, 135, 136, 137, 138, 139, 140, 141, 142, 143, 147, 150, 154,
    157, 158, 160, 162, 163, 164, 165, 168
Wood, Beverly, 13, 17, 19, 20, 22, 60, 159, 160, 168
Wood, Hodge, xi, xii, 13, 15, 16, 21, 37, 45, 50, 61, 72, 78, 80, 85, 89, 94, 95,
    101, 109, 110, 116, 121, 126, 127, 145, 155, 158
Wood, John, 2, 28, 60, 74
wreck, 2, 3, 5, 7, 23, 40, 57, 65, 77, 84, 86, 87, 132, 141, 142, 152, 161

YMCA, 70
    Young Mens Christian Association